P9-DUH-619

CONTENTS

CONTENTS

CONTENTS

CONTENTS

SCHOOL FINANCE: A CALIFORNIA PERSPECTIVE

SIXTH EDITION

ARTHUR J. TOWNLEY

Professor Emeritus
School of Education
California State University, San Bernardino

JUNE H. SCHMIEDER-RAMIREZ

Professor
School of Education & Psychology
Pepperdine University, California

LILLIAN B. WEHMEYER

Professor
School of Education & Behavioral Studies
Azusa Pacific University, California

KENDALL/HUNT PUBLISHING COMPANY
4050 Westmark Drive   Dubuque, Iowa 52002

CONTENTS

Contents

CONTENTS

CONTENTS

LIST OF FIGURES

LIST OF TABLES

INTRODUCTION

California school finance has the same reputation as quantum physics—very complex. The objective of this book is to illuminate a path through the thicket of financial terms and present the subject in a straightforward way.

California school finance has endured tremendous upheaval in the last two decades. Meeting the educational needs of an increasing and diverse student population remains a major challenge for the citizens of this state. Many school districts in California, particularly those in urban populations and those declining in enrollment, must constantly reduce some programs to meet increasing demands in others. Districts continually seek expanded resources to balance the budget and maintain a viable educational program. Among the causes of this never-ending quest are collective bargaining settlements, need for new facilities, and deteriorating assets.

For many years, California depended upon the property tax to finance schools. Districts in neighboring communities had been spending unequal amounts per student to accomplish similar educational goals. However, in a landmark case that reversed this traditional means of state school financing, the 1971 *Serrano* decision declared the property tax unconstitutional as a means of supporting public schools (*Serrano v. Priest*, upheld 18 C.3d 728 [1976]). The court ruled that neither a child's place of residence nor the wealth of a community should determine financial support for the educational program.

Beginning in 1972, several school bills were passed to implement *Serrano*, and subsequently, to recover the dollars lost in the wake of Proposition 13. Nevertheless, in 1999-2000 the per-pupil expenditure in California was less than the amount spent per child in 41 states, including New York, Illinois, Michigan, Massachusetts, and Pennsylvania. What has emerged in California school finance is strong state control of funds—and consequently of educational programs. Local school boards find themselves without means to raise revenue or to build facilities. They have become almost totally dependent upon actions in Sacramento.

The information presented in this book is as up-to-date as possible. Nevertheless, because school finance is continually evolving, any book on this topic must inevitably contain some inaccuracies, even before it can be printed. Therefore, the reader will find it necessary to keep track of developments ranging from local bond elections to state and federal legislation and court decisions affecting local school districts.

Topics included in this text are a history of school finance, the evolving environment of California education, income and expenditure analysis, and school facility laws. Other sections discuss budget development, projection of school district revenues and expenditures, and financial reporting. Also addressed are the roles of the chief business official (CBO), maintenance and operations, school transportation, food services, program budgeting, and a glossary of school finance terms.

SPECIAL OFFER
to
INSTRUCTORS/PROFESSORS
who teach school finance/management

* Class notes for overheads can be obtained at Dr. Townley's Website:
http://soe.csusb.edu/atownley

* If you would like a copy of Dr. Townley's school finance examinations,
please contact him at atownle2@juno.com

CHAPTER 1

FINANCING EDUCATION
IN AN ATMOSPHERE OF CHANGE

INTRODUCTION

Anyone who has followed educational debates in the press, attended a school board meeting, or listened to a discussion among educators knows there is little consensus on the ends of education or how to achieve them. Compounding this issue is the realization that education is "big business," with one person in five either attending or employed by a secondary or elementary school.

Nevertheless, certain broad educational goals may be agreed upon by most citizens. For example, many would agree that education should prepare the student to do meaningful work and to become a productive member of society in the United States. Beyond this obvious agreement, however, lies a host of issues: individual versus group goals, religious versus secular emphases, vocational versus general skills, and debates over allocation of precious resources to achieve the greatest benefit.

DEBATES AND DILEMMAS IN SCHOOL FINANCE

Despite the consensus among most Americans that education is top priority, many issues remain unresolved. For example, arguments have raged for years about patterns of school district organization. How should districts and schools be organized to promote equality of educational outcomes? Should the desires of the community take precedence over those of the district, state, or nation in governance of the local school? How do concerns for competition in the global economy or pressures for school choice impact the future of schooling? What is the proper role of the federal government in K-12 education?

The two purposes of this chapter are to raise issues that frame major educational dilemmas facing the profession and to propose elements of policy on which we seem to agree. The latter center around the value of education for both the individual and the public. Those issues on which we lack consensus relate to linking resources to outcomes and a funding structure that will best deliver those resources. These provocative issues provide a backdrop for delving into the great issues in educational finance.

WIDELY ACCEPTED CONCEPTS

Even though competing social values cloud issues of school finance, several concepts are widely accepted. These concepts include:

- the private and the public good of education
- local autonomy
- fiscal federalism
- funding for special needs
- equal opportunity
- efficiency.

PRIVATE AND PUBLIC GOOD OF EDUCATION. There are many reasons why education is regarded as a public good. The main argument involves the benefit to society of an educated populace. An educated citizenry is better able to cast informed votes, manage personal resources, and benefit from lifelong learning. The return to society from an educated populace was thoroughly discussed in 1776 by Adam Smith in *The Wealth of Nations* and further developed by Charles Benson in 1978.

Closely tied to the argument of the value of an educated populace are the consequences of an uneducated citizenry. The major costs of welfare are well documented. In addition, studies have compared the cost of one year in prison with the cost of one year of preschool—a shocking illustration of the price of failure to fund education, especially at the pre-kindergarten level. Of course, it must be acknowledged that numerous other factors are related to crime and unemployment, including individual characteristics, early upbringing, opportunity, and determination.

Turning to education as a private good, many studies have illustrated the benefit of education over a lifetime of earnings. Furthermore, state courts have upheld the right of each individual to an education. Although an individual acquires benefits from an education, so do the nation, state, local community, employers, and taxpayers. Consequently, a debate arises as to who should pay for this benefit. Even if it is agreed that all should share the burden of financing education, further contention centers on precisely how that burden should be distributed.

LOCAL AUTONOMY. Within districts, a traditional approach to budgeting has placed salary and fringe benefit decisions at the central office, allocating a limited amount to local sites for instructional supplies and supplementary services. This approach has been prevalent because the district retains the capacity to track personnel expenditures—the highest line item in the budget.

However, decentralization of school district leadership emerged as a major thrust in the 1990s as public schools sought to respond to negative public perceptions. Urban school districts, which have languished in search of superintendents to lead them, are adopting local autonomy as a way to increase school productivity. The concept that underlies school-based management is that decisions are typically based on better information when they are made close to the level at which they are implemented.

Even though the overall purpose of local autonomy is to delegate more power to local schools, site-based management has many variations. Districts differ widely in the degree to which decentralization and local autonomy are instituted. Most approaches to decentralization involve empowerment of groups that include parents, teachers, and—at the secondary level—students. Site-based management and its variants have been the subject of multitudinous conferences throughout the state.

FISCAL FEDERALISM. The funding relationship among local, state, and federal governments has been described as a marbled layer cake that miraculously works, although in a cumbersome manner. "Fiscal federalism" is the formal term for this relationship. It involves a balancing act among the levels of government. For example, in cases of wide disparity in funding for local districts, the state can step in to compensate for regional differences in amounts allocated per pupil. Similarly, the federal government may supplement budgets for special needs such as special education and compensatory education.

FUNDING FOR SPECIAL NEEDS. One basic tenet of American education is the concept of vertical equity. Because not all students have the same educational needs, funds must be provided to supplement the minimal amount allocated to each child. For example, children who score at a particularly low level on standardized tests are eligible for additional revenue. Special education children and the gifted and talented are also allotted additional funds in California.

Disagreements have arisen as to the amount of funding necessary for children with special needs. Some superintendents have argued that insufficient funds are allocated for special education students and that counties are skimming an inordinate amount of indirect cost off the top of district allotments.

Another group with special needs, students for whom English is a second language, is not a new concern. Indeed, heated discussion ensued as each wave of immigrants reached our shores. Educators at all levels have argued about the responsibility of public schools to accept newcomers and the language in which their education is best provided. This debate can be expected to continue for several generations.

EQUAL OPPORTUNITY. A typical third-grade teacher in California may have several students with special needs. One pupil may be physically handicapped, while another needs additional reading instruction. Some students may have visited London and Paris, yet other students have not traveled more than six blocks from home. The concept of equal opportunity plays an important role in these scenarios. Equal educational opportunity is based on the recognition that students have widely varying needs and abilities and the principle that school services should be linked to each student according to these requirements. Additional or adaptive services should be available to students who need them. Compensatory education and special education services are well-known programs intended to ensure equality of educational opportunity.

EFFICIENCY. The general public's desire for efficiency in the educational system is paralleled in the business community. Yet efficiency is extremely difficult to measure. Even within the profession, not to mention the communities our schools serve, we find disagreement on the actual product or outcome to be measured, concern over the ambiguous nature of "human output," confusion on the linkage of inputs to outcomes, and consequently, difficulty in determining cost-effectiveness.

SCHOOL FINANCE ISSUES UNDER DEBATE

Even though the responsible public agrees on the importance of education, disagreement abounds as to methods of taxation, alternative sources of income, and appropriate linkages between resources and students. Taxpayer revolts are a manifestation of disagreement on the best way to fund education.

In this section, major points of disagreement in school finance are discussed. Dilemmas to be addressed include:

- forms of taxation
- the voucher/choice/privatization issue
- the federal role in education
- the point of diminishing returns

- student assessment
- linkage of resources to outcomes
- alternative funding sources
- myths about money for schools.

FORMS OF TAXATION. The choice of taxation that should support the educational system has been hotly debated. Most observers feel that a progressive tax system is most effective—one that increases the tax on individuals as their income rises. If the public determines that a tax is too heavy a burden, there follows a critical event such as the passage of Proposition 13, the tax revolt initiative in California in the late 1970s.

Characteristics of an ideal tax include production of consistent revenues, equity to those taxed, and ease of administration. Table 1 summarizes the major advantages and disadvantages of various taxes.

Even though the property tax was historically the major source of school revenues, it has not been without problems. Property assessment practices have been confusing, and the local aspect of the tax has been deemed unfair in some instances. The wide variation in tax-base wealth among local school districts is well documented in the literature.

Table 1
Major Advantages and Disadvantages
of Various Taxes

Tax	Advantages	Disadvantages
Income Tax	Increases in amount in economically healthy periods Increases vertical equity	Decreases in amount in periods of economic slowdown Sometimes expensive to administer and monitor
Sales Tax	Inexpensive to implement Increases in amount in economically healthy periods	Regressive, i.e., becomes a burden on those least able to pay Decreases in amount in periods of economic slowdown
Property Tax	Usually consistent in periods of economic slowdown Ease of identifying the taxpayer	Perplexing equity issues Sometimes a burden for lower-income homeowners

The sales tax has been another means of obtaining revenue. It is easy to monitor and creates less public outcry than property taxes. However, the sales tax is classified as regressive because it sometimes collects most from those who can least afford to support the financial burden of public education.

THE VOUCHER/CHOICE/PRIVATIZATION ISSUE. The most hotly disputed issue of the 1990s was school choice, partly because it received national attention. But choice is not a new issue. Since the founding of the educational system, it has often been discussed and debated. In particular, the private and public sectors have been at odds over this question, which remains on the national agenda as the 21st century moves forward.

The voucher is a manifestation of school choice that involves issuance of a document entitling the student to schooling of family preference. As a proposition on the California ballot, the voucher initiative has not garnered enough public approval to pass, even though much effort has been expended in its behalf. An advantage advanced by voucher proponents is that the system gives families more influence over their children's education. This influence, they argue, would eventually generate market forces that would drive public schools to change for the better. One disadvantage, according to critics, is that the voucher would erode even further the low level of financial support for public education.

THE FEDERAL ROLE IN EDUCATION. There was little debate about the federal government's role in K-12 education until the second half of the 20th century. Prior to the 1950s, the U. S. Department of Health, Education, and Welfare exerted little influence over funding and management of education, which was regarded as a responsibility of the states. However, Congress and American citizens received a shock in 1957 when the Soviet Union launched Sputnik. This unexpected event resulted in passage and funding of the National Defense Education Act of 1958, legislation that provided federal support for education at all levels, from kindergarten to higher education.

Further expansion of the federal government's role in education took place under the leadership of President Lyndon Johnson. With Johnson's concept of "the Great Society," the school lunch program initiated under President Truman was expanded and a series of laws approved and funded to promote education. Funds were made available for a variety of programs, including monies for states to improve achievement of educationally disadvantaged students. Head Start was promoted for preschool children, and funds were made available for school libraries. Then, under

President Carter, a separate cabinet post was created for education, and the Office of Education became the U. S. Department of Education.

During most of the first half of the 20th century, support for federal intervention in education was divided along party lines, with Republicans generally opposing federal education programs and Democrats supporting the concept. The disagreement reached its zenith with the election of President Reagan, who threatened to abolish the Department of Education.

However, the early 1990s saw a major shift of educational policy in the Republican Party when President George Bush supported Goals 2000, originally developed by the governors of the 50 states. No further mention was made of abolishing the Department of Education. In the election of 2000, when Al Gore faced off against George W. Bush, both Democrats and Republicans embraced support for education. Bush listed education as his number one priority, dramatized by the slogan: "No child shall be left behind." His support moved from slogan to reality as the education budget saw an increase from President Clinton's last education budget of $40 million to $169 million. Consequently, disagreement as to whether the federal government has a role in education may give way to disagreement as to the extent of involvement and its form.

THE POINT OF DIMINISHING RETURNS. One classic question is fascinating to discuss: What is the point beyond which additional expenditures yield little or no increased educational returns? This issue can realistically be called the "mystery spot" of public education. The point is theoretical, since there is no precise agreement on educational outcomes. Nevertheless, it is assumed that most educational systems in the United States are at a point far below any risk of no return, simply because financial support for education has eroded in recent years.

Nevertheless, this has been a popular topic for research papers for decades. For example, while an expenditure of $6,000 may be deemed appropriate for each child in one state, $7,000 may be seen as the desirable amount in another. The additional $1,000 per pupil may mean taking funds away from other government goods and services, thus opening fresh subjects for discussion.

STUDENT ASSESSMENT. A central principle of George W. Bush's plan for education included increased accountability through national and state testing. Under his plan, each child would be tested in math and reading in grades 3 through 8. In addition, each state would be required to administer the National Assessment of Educational Progress to a limited sample of fourth- and eighth-grade students.

These proposals engendered sharp disagreement centered around a number of issues:

- What are the effectiveness and value of assessment?
- Should the federal government mandate a national test?
- Is testing/assessment the first step to a national curriculum? If so, is that desirable?
- What happens to low-performing schools?
- Is testing/assessment the first step to a voucher system?
- Does testing/assessment lead to improved learning or achievement? More specifically, will student performance be improved, or will teachers teach to the test?
- Can equity issues be resolved by national assessment?

The concept of national student assessment will continue to be debated at national, state, and local levels. Teachers have high stakes in the debate since some states, including California, have provided financial incentives to teachers whose students show significant achievement as measured by standardized tests. Students will also be involved in the debate about their future, determined in part by achievement on the tests. As this text goes to press, students in Scarsdale, New York, made national news by boycotting a state science exam—with their parents' blessing. This boycott is part of a nationwide movement against tests; similar demonstrations have also occurred in Michigan and Massachusetts.

LINKING EXPENDITURES TO STUDENT OUTCOMES. The concept of "educational productivity" is gaining ground. The belief that schools need to increase student achievement, and that achievement is directly related to expenditures, has become widespread across the nation. Allocating financial resources to education is a responsibility of federal, state, and local lawmakers. However, procedures for determining these allocations have been ambiguous, subject to varied interpretations. At times, governmental bodies have distributed resources based upon political expediency. In such an environment, education may be at a disadvantage because of the difficulty of measuring increased output as a consequence of additional input.

Policymakers must decide what aspects of student achievement are the school's responsibility and what factors, such as student poverty, are beyond the school's control or outside the school's responsibility. As a result of this emphasis on accountability, educators are coming to realize that they must be attentive to all their clients, including parents, community members, and individual politicians.

ALTERNATIVE FUNDING SOURCES. A potentially exciting area of study is that of alternative funding sources. These are sources that have typically not been tapped in the past. Many have caused a flood of controversy, even though, like the "use tax," they have not been applied to any great extent.

Site-Value Tax. This is a tax on the actual value of land, even though it may be unimproved. As the value of the land appreciates, the tax increases. Other countries use this system with good results.

Value-added Tax. In its clearest form, VAT is a tax on the value of goods at each transaction level, from production to consumption. The tax can be levied on each good or service at each stage.

Lottery. In 1989 lotteries were run in 33 states plus the District of Columbia. Their popularity probably lies in the low price of the tickets coupled with the hope that one might become wealthy. Studies have shown that most purchasers of lottery tickets are either poor or middle class.

In California, 34 cents out of every lottery dollar are allocated to education. This sounds like a large proportion; however, the lottery has not provided the windfall for education that some expected. Lottery monies typically constitute only 2% to 3% of a school district's revenue. In addition, school officials at the state level sometimes draw on lottery income to supplement state allotments.

Private Foundations. The private sector is proving a fertile ground for development of new revenue sources. Private foundations established in connection with a school district have met with mixed results. Their success depends to a great extent upon the wealth of community members, although motivated educators have sparked increased giving in some low-income districts.

School-Business Partnerships. Partnerships between schools and businesses are not completely altruistic, as both sides typically benefit. However, both partners seek the same goal—to prepare students for the 21st century. In the most successful partnerships, a business works directly with the school it is supporting. Many schools report success with businesses operating within a five-mile radius. An example of a creative partnership is that of a Los Angeles high school class that has succeeded at selling salad dressing, made as part of a class project, in local grocery stores.

MYTHS ABOUT MONEY FOR SCHOOLS. Two hotly debated myths about money and schooling have clouded public discussion of finance for schools. The first of these is that the United States spends more money on its schools than any other nation in the world. This myth was widely disseminated during the George Bush administration. The second myth is that money makes no difference in student achievement. These two myths are so prevalent that they are quoted from backyard fences to the corridors of Congress.

Bracey (1995) debunks these myths by marshaling some interesting facts. First, he calculated the dollars spent annually per student in the world's 16 most prosperous nations. Among these countries the United States was only average in per-student expenditures. Moreover, when spending was calculated in relationship to per capita income, the U. S. finished 14th among the 16 countries. Bracey further contends that even this ranking is misleading because in the United States a smaller proportion of appropriated funds actually reaches classrooms. He supports this contention by asserting that American schools provide services that other countries either do not provide at all or provide to a lesser extent. In addition to classroom expenditures, the U. S. spends education dollars on food service, transportation, counselors, special education, and so on. Consequently, the U. S. is the only nation of the 16 in which less than 50% of school employees are classroom teachers.

The second myth, that there is no relationship between money and achievement, is coupled with a belief that the United States has been spending more money without a commensurate gain in test scores. First, is it true that U. S. spent more money on education during the 1980s than in previous decades? Rothstein of the Economic Policy Institute (1995) contends that although more money was spent on education during this period, very little of it went to general education classrooms. Rothstein's calculations span the years from 1965, when average spending was $2,611 per pupil (in 1990 dollars), to 1990, when spending was $5,251 per student. He found that nearly 30% of the increase went into special education, while 10% was spent for school breakfast and lunch programs. Transportation absorbed 5%, while another 3% was directed to dropout reduction programs. Of the remainder, 30% was utilized to reduce class size and 21% went into salary increases.

Second, is it true that expenditures are unrelated to pupil achievement? Wainer of Educational Testing Service (1993) investigated this issue and found a significant correlation between NAEP scores and per-pupil expenditures. In addition, Bracey (1995) cites districts noted for high student achievement and the large amount of money spent per student. For example, schools in Jericho, New York, spent $15,989 per pupil in 1991-92, while New York City spent only $6,981. The widely acclaimed New Trier High School in Illinois spent $12,198 in that year, while the state of Illinois averaged $5,036.

An example of a state that increased funds for education and improved student achievement is Connecticut. In 1996 Connecticut raised educational expenditures by $300 million. The additional funds were used to increase teacher salaries, improve teacher training, and purchase instructional books and supplies. By 1998 the state had the highest average reading scores in the nation in the fourth and eighth grades and in 1999, the highest scores in writing (Donahue, 2000).

LOOKING AHEAD

Four tenets set a foundation for future directions in school finance:

1. The cost of education will continue to escalate. If California persists in placing education near the bottom of its funding priorities, the mismatch between rising costs and low student achievement will create an unresolvable dilemma.

2. The economic and cultural conditions of students will continue to affect their educational attainment. This relationship will impact the funding required to bring all students to a "level playing field."

3. Differences among students in ability, interest, and the desire to attain graduation will continue to complicate the process of allocating resources to education.

4. There is no disagreement concerning the economic or non-economic benefits of education. Educational attainment is tied to future earnings, and non-economic benefits are considerable.

State priorities will impact the first point to a great degree. If California experiences an economic downturn in any given year, this decline directly affects funds allocated to students. Since the tenth amendment determines that education is a state responsibility, the actions of the legislature must be monitored closely.

Secondly, the economic and cultural milieu of students has powerful impact on their educational attainment. In its "report card" on California's children, Children Now (1996) reported that "compared with 1960, American children in 1992 spent an average of 10 to 12 hours less time per week with their parents." A fifth of California children—nearly two million—lacked health insurance, and uninsured children were less likely to be taken to a doctor when needed. Data on family income levels suggest that 37% of California children may be suffering hunger.

The third issue, differential ability among students, affects the quantity of resources necessary to educate them. Attempts will continue to be made to assign more resources to underachieving schools in the hope of giving their pupils an opportunity to graduate from high school. Differential resources will also continue to be necessary for students with special physical needs and language requirements. Another debatable issue: How much should the federal government subsidize these costs?

There are no arguments regarding the fourth point—that education brings economic and non-economic benefits. Each year of education can be tied to a higher average future earnings figure that is hard to dispute. Opponents to revenue increases need to consider the long-term costs when education is not provided. It is interesting to note that with few exceptions, states with the lowest dropout rate have the lowest rate of prisoners per 100,000 people. Where, then, should monies be invested: in prisons, welfare plans, law enforcement, or education?

California citizens are generally committed to the importance of public education. In a 1997 public opinion survey, 32% of voters cited elementary and secondary education as the state's greatest problem, followed by crime and drugs at 22% and immigration, named by 12% (Herdt, 1997).

An optimistic observation with implications for the future of education is that most parents of school-age children are happy with their neighborhood school. They realize that, as expensive as public education may be, the cost to society of not educating its people is far higher. The detrimental societal effect of illiteracy, welfare, and prison occupancy is untenable in the long term. Considering the lifelong return in earnings and the large investment already made, California must provide the best education for its youth, regardless of their place of residence, the affluence of their parents, or the economic wealth of the school district.

SUMMARY

Most American citizens support public education. Since the end of the "Cold War," education has moved to become the top or near their top priority. Despite a general consensus that education needs to be reformed and improved, however, the meaning of "reformed" and "improved" is unclear. Older citizens yearn for the "good old days," with an emphasis on citizenship and the "three Rs," while others expand on "thinking outside the box." Managers of national and international enterprises bemoan the lack of skills among employees, while artists and musicians decry the lack of culture in the schools.

Educational debate reached a zenith at the national level in the presidential campaign of 2000 between Al Gore and George W. Bush, with each candidate promising to be "The Education President." Debate centered around a number of issues, including school choice, national assessment, and the amount of federal financial support for education. It is predicted that education will continue as a major priority of American citizens well into the 21st century, with ongoing debate on the goals of education and its financial support.

KEY TERMS

Alternative funding
Diminishing return
Equity & efficiency
Fiscal federalism
Income tax
Local autonomy
Private & public good of education
Private foundation

Property tax
Sales tax
School-business partnerships
Site-value tax
Special needs
Value-Added Tax (VAT)
Voucher/choice/privatization

DISCUSSION/ESSAY QUESTIONS

1. Discuss three major arguments in support of "the public good of education."

2. Equity and efficiency are desirable goals of American public education. Briefly define each term. Discuss the goal you feel is most achievable. Explain your answer.

3. Schools are supported by several sources of tax dollars. Which of the modes of taxation do you feel is most advantageous for supporting public education? Why?

4. "Choice" continues to be hotly debated in the 21st century. What are the advantages and disadvantages of providing parents with a choice of public school?

5. Support for public education will remain a major topic of discussion among educators, the public, and legislative bodies. Discuss the tenets that will continue to underlie school finance challenges during the next decade.

CHAPTER 2

HISTORY OF CALIFORNIA SCHOOL FINANCE

INTRODUCTION

The story of formal education in California begins with the Franciscan missions. For pupils other than Indians, 55 schools were established during the Spanish and Mexican periods (Caughey, 1943). All were elementary schools, and most of them functioned only briefly. On April 3, 1848, San Francisco established the first California public school, taught by Thomas Douglas. Two months later, four of the five trustees, several students, and schoolmaster Douglas abandoned the school and left for the goldfields.

With growing population and California statehood in 1850, the demand for public schools accelerated. Reflecting this demand, the first state constitution required the legislature to provide for a school in each district in the state. However, the school was only required to operate three months per year. San Francisco again took the lead and opened its first public high school in 1856 (Caughey, 1943). Between 1850 and the early 1900s, as California's population expanded, the number of public schools increased.

During the second half of the 19th century, California school districts and communities struggled to provide facilities, equipment, and staff for public schools. This struggle was often taken out of the control of school boards and citizens in the local districts. Rather, the state legislature and the courts played a dominant role in control and finance of public education. In addition, citizens of California have often relied on the initiative process to provide direction to school curriculum and funding. This chapter highlights those major court cases, propositions, legislation, and events that have influenced public education in California.

STUDENT POPULATION

As the richest state in the West, California could afford to finance public schools. As of 1940, the state's per capita expenditure was exceeded only by that of New York. Nevertheless, California experienced ongoing difficulties in providing adequate financing for public education. The situation was exacerbated by the rapid increase in school population, which more than doubled between 1914 and 1940.

With the coming of World War II, California school districts were again overwhelmed by a tremendous increase in population. School districts in the vicinity of war plants and military bases were confronted with a sudden increase in enrollment, far beyond any expectations. To cope with increased enrollment, some districts constructed completely new schools. Other districts, however, had to rely on crowding more students into existing buildings, often forcing schools and teachers do double duty through half-day sessions.

In the year 2000, one out of every eight children in the United States lived in California. With a public school K-12 enrollment of 5,951,612 in the fall of 1999, California exceeded all other states (California Department of Education, 2000a). The second largest school population was that of Texas, with an enrollment of 4,002,227 (Texas Department of Education, 2000). To illustrate the size of student enrollment, more students are enrolled in California's public schools than the combined total populations at the last census of Wyoming, Vermont, District of Columbia, Alaska, North Dakota, Delaware, South Dakota, and Montana (U. S. Bureau of the Census, 2000).

SECOND HALF OF THE 20TH CENTURY

During the second half of the 20th century, a series of court decisions, propositions, and legislation resulted in a shift from property taxes to other forms of taxation as the primary source of funds for education in California. This change resulted, to a significant degree, in transferring local control of education to state control. With this change, school finance became much more complex.

Public education has also been greatly influenced by California's governors and the priority each has placed on education. As the 20th century drew to a close, Governors Pete Wilson and Gray Davis both ran on platforms supporting public education. Davis, elected in 1998, introduced a series of educational reforms that have greatly impacted education. This chapter provides a historical perspective by discussing major legal actions affecting education, including the court decision in *Serrano v. Priest*, Senate Bill 90, Proposition 13, the Gann Limit, Senate Bill 813, Proposition 37, Proposition 98, Proposition 111, Senate Bills 1977 and 376, and Proposition 227.

1968—*SERRANO V. PRIEST*

Prior to 1972, school district finances were largely dependent upon property taxes, which furnished about 2/3 of education revenues during those years. Since these taxes were determined by the city or other legal entity in which the taxpayer lived, per-pupil resources for education varied widely. Reliance on local property taxes as a major source of school revenues inevitably produces fiscal inequities because the property tax base is not distributed equally across school districts. As a result, property-poor districts usually have low resources and expenditures per pupil, even when they levy a high tax rate. By the same token, property-rich districts usually enjoy high resources and expenditures per pupil, even with a low tax rate. At the time the *Serrano* suit was brought to court, educational expenditures per student ranged from $274 in one California district to $1,710 in another, a ratio of 6.2:1.

In 1968 a group of attorneys brought suit in the California courts in behalf of John Serrano against Ivy Baker Priest, who was California's State Treasurer at that time. John Serrano was a student enrolled in Baldwin Park School District, a low-revenue district. At that time, Baldwin Park was spending $577 per student, while the Beverly Hills school district was spending $1,223. This inequity was due to the difference in assessed valuation of property per pupil in the two districts: $50,885 in Beverly Hills and $3,706 in Baldwin Park, a ratio of nearly 14:1. The school tax rate paid in the two districts revealed a reverse inequity: Baldwin Park taxpayers were paying $5.48 per $100 of assessed valuation while Beverly Hills residents paid only $2.38 per $100. Attorneys for Serrano argued that the 14th Amendment to the U. S. Constitution and the Education Clause of the California Constitution made it unconstitutional for local property wealth to be linked to school revenues per pupil.

The California Supreme Court decided the case in favor of the plaintiff. In upholding the *Serrano* decision, the California Supreme Court held that the state tax system violated the right of students to receive an equal education.

1972—SENATE BILL 90

In 1972 the State of California enacted SB (Senate Bill) 90, which limited the maximum amount of general purpose state and local revenues a local district could receive. The revenue limit formula set a base amount per student, added an adjustment for students with special needs, and further increased the limit in response to inflation. The key equalization feature was an adjustment that provided a higher dollar amount to low-revenue districts. As SB 90 was implemented, high-revenue districts found their revenue limits leveling down toward a statewide average. Yet in 1974, a California Superior Court ruled that progress toward equalization was too little and too slow. The court decreed that disparities must decrease at a faster rate. Finally, 15 years later, in 1989, the California Appellate Court ruled that satisfactory progress had been made, and the case was closed.

Without the court mandate, the state has continued to provide extra funds for low-revenue districts, eventually bringing them up to the statewide average. A record 79.9% of students came within the allowable range of $324 in 1997-98 (Goldfinger, 2001).

1978—PROPOSITION 13

When voters approved Proposition 13, also known as the Jarvis Amendment, they created massive changes in school funding in California. The leaders of this tax revolt, Howard Jarvis and Paul Gann, dramatically changed the system of taxation in this state and, eventually, nationwide. The two men were an odd couple who shared a vision of lower property taxes. Jarvis's background was as publisher of a small newspaper in Utah; in the early 1960s he moved to Southern California, where he became a political anti-tax crusader. Gann, a preacher's son, quoted Biblical passages in a soothing drawl that was reminiscent of his Arkansas roots.

With successful passage of Proposition 13, Howard Jarvis became a celebrity. He appeared on talk shows, his picture was featured on the cover of *Time* magazine, and his success resulted in Proposition 13-type tax revolts in other parts of the country.

The problem of ever-increasing property taxes in California had been real. The 1960s and 1970s were a time of escalating inflation in California, particularly acute in the cost of homes. One of the authors of this text purchased a home in 1964 for $23,000 and saw the price double within a three-year period, along with a like increase in the assessed value and property tax. Some retirees could not afford their property tax bills and faced the prospect of having to sell homes they had purchased after World War II.

However, although Proposition 13 rolled back property taxes, it had unintended consequences. It did much more than change California's property tax system. California politics would never be the same. Today, almost all California tax dollars flow to Sacramento, where the state takes its cut, then sends what is left back to school districts, counties, and cities. But that is not all. The state legislature, much like an autocratic father, not only distributes the money, but also decrees how it will be spent. The most dramatic and far-reaching effect of Proposition 13 was to shift power in education from local school districts and municipalities to Sacramento.

Proposition 13 resulted in a generation of leaders dead set against raising taxes, and it was a boon for homeowners and businesses. The initiative immediately cut taxes by more than 50%, or $6.1 billion, statewide. This tax revolt became an American way of life long after the two tax crusaders left the scene. Politically, cutting taxes has been popular in state and national battles for Congress and the White House. Some political analysts attribute a major cause of President George Bush's defeat in 1992 to his famous "Read my lips: no new taxes" statement—a promise that, as it turned out, he was unable to keep. Cutting taxes was also a major campaign issue in 2000 between Vice-president Al Gore and Texas Governor George W. Bush.

Proposition 13 imposed a 1% limit on general purpose property tax rates, calculated either on the 1975-76 value of the property plus a maximum 2% annual inflation increase or on the purchase price upon sale. When a district computes its revenue limit, it may find its share of the 1% to be higher or lower than its calculated revenue limit. If the tax share exceeds the revenue limit, the latter is subtracted from the former, and the difference reverts to the state. If there is a shortfall, the state allocates funds to ensure that the district receives its per-pupil revenue limit.

A growing concern in consequence of Proposition 13 focuses on the unequal collection of taxes on similar, neighboring properties. A property that is sold becomes taxable on its selling price, thus generating a higher tax bill than one subject only to the 2% annual increase. Earlier, the California Supreme Court had refused to hear three cases on the subject. However, in the spring of 1991 the U. S. Supreme Court accepted a suit by Macy's department store. The suit was withdrawn by Macy's, but the court agreed to decide a similar suit brought by a Los Angeles homeowner (*Nordlinger v. Hahn,* Case No 90-1912). The plaintiff, Stephanie Nordlinger, argued that Proposition 13 violated equal protection under the law, as stipulated in the 14th amendment to the federal constitution. Ms. Nordlinger, who purchased a house in 1988 for $170,000, was paying about $1,700 a year in property taxes. Nordlinger's neighbors, who had owned similar houses before Proposition 13 went into effect, paid $350 to $400 per year.

In June 1992 the U. S. Supreme Court ruled that Proposition 13 was legal. Although the ruling called the property tax system distasteful and unwise, the court refused to upset the will of the people of California as expressed in Proposition 13. In an eight-to-one ruling, the court said Proposition 13 does not violate the U. S. Constitutional guarantee of equal protection under the law, even though it grants tax relief to longtime residents at the expense of new homeowners. Justice Harry A. Blackburn, writing for the court, said, "The states have a large leeway in making classifications for tax purposes as long as they do not discriminate against a particular group, such as blacks or women" (Savage, 1992).

The major impact of Proposition 13 is the higher level of state aid now in the formula. As a result, K-12 education has become almost totally dependent upon fluctuations in the state economy, instead of the more reliable property tax. Anything that has a negative impact on state revenues, such as the earthquakes in San Francisco, Landers, and San Fernando or the enormous cost of electrical energy in response to the shortage of 2001, has negative impact on the state's ability to fund education.

1979—GANN LIMIT

As part of the "taxpayers' revolt" in the late 70s, the Gann limit was approved in November of 1979 in the form of Proposition 4. This constitutional amendment established limits on allowable growth in state and local government spending. The limits permit government spending to increase at a rate no faster than inflation and the change in population. The result of this amendment was to make state spending an ever-decreasing percentage of personal income. The Gann limit created a "squeeze" on resources available to local school districts in addition to that previously generated by Proposition 13.

1983—SENATE BILL 813

School funding improved in 1983-84. This improvement resulted in part from the fact that the 1982-83 recession was of short duration, so that the state economy grew strongly in 1983-84. The second reason for improvement was that educators, parents, and business leaders formed a coalition that accomplished passage of SB 813, known as the Hughes/Hart Education Reform Act.

This bill marked the first step after *Serrano* toward rehabilitation of education in California. Programs were implemented to increase the length of the school year and the school day, the mentor teacher program was instituted, and beginning teachers' salaries were improved. Other reforms included mini-grants for teachers, funding for instructional materials, and increased counseling for high school sophomores. However, even with these changes, California still ranked below the national average in per-pupil expenditures for education.

1984—PROPOSITION 37: CALIFORNIA STATE LOTTERY

The California State Lottery Act (Proposition 37) was approved by the voters in 1984 and implemented by the state legislature in 1985. The Lottery Act states that the purpose of the California lottery is to generate funding to supplement the public education budget to the extent of at least 34% of sales. Additional lottery information is included in Chapter 5—Developing the Budget.

1988—PROPOSITION 98

Proposition 98 was approved by voters in November of 1988—again as a result of joint effort by parents and educators, including the California Teachers' Association. This proposition established a constitutionally-based, minimum funding floor for K-14 education. Proposition 98 retains education's first right to state revenues. Proposition 98 includes the following provisions:

- maintenance of a sufficient reserve by the state
- adoption of a "School Accountability Report Card," which details student achievement, dropout rate, class size, and similar items
- a formula that adjusts revenue allocations beyond the Gann limitations
- minimum base funding (40.33% of tax revenue) for K-14 education.

Proposition 98, as subsequently modified by Proposition 111 (see next section), contains three tests to determine minimum base funding for public schools:

- **Test 1** requires the state to allocate to K-14 school districts at least 34.55% of state general fund taxes. This is equal to the percentage set in 1986-87, but adjusted for the property tax shift to K-14 districts.

- **Test 2** requires that districts receive at least the same amount of state aid and local tax dollars as in the prior year, plus statewide K-12 ADA growth and an inflation factor equal to the annual percentage change in per capita personal income.

- **Test 3** was added with the passage of Proposition 111 in 1990. It states that when growth in state taxes per capita plus 1/2% is less than growth in California personal income per capita, then the Test 2 inflation factor is reduced to growth in state taxes per capita plus 1/2%.

The effect of these tests depends on state revenues, local property taxes, enrollment growth, personal income, and state population. Proposition 98 minimum funding level is generally calculated under Test 2, which is unrelated to current economic factors. However, in very good economic years, Test 1 applies, while in a very bad economic period, such as the recession years in the early 1990s, Test 3 applies. The proposition also includes a provision that allows the state to suspend base funding provisions for one year by enacting urgency legislation. Such a suspension requires a 2/3 vote in both houses of the legislature and the signature of the governor.

Proposition 98 has eliminated competition for direct funding between education and other programs. It also modified the Gann Limit. Should the state ever again receive tax revenues in excess of its Gann limit, 50% of that excess amount will be allocated in that year to K-14 school districts on the basis of equal dollars per ADA, up to a maximum of 40% of the agency's prior year base funding. Gann limit excess revenues may be used only for the following five areas:

- class size reduction to not more than 20 students per class and a total teacher load of 100 students per teacher
- instructional supplies, equipment, or materials
- direct services to students to ensure academic progress
- staff development programs designed primarily by classroom teachers, or
- teacher compensation.

1990—PROPOSITION 111

Proposition 111 was approved by California voters in June of 1990. Although this proposition was called "The Traffic Congestion Relief and Spending Limitation Act of 1990," popularly referred to as the "gas tax," it contained several provisions regarding funds for education. In addition to continuing to provide public education and community colleges with at least 40% of the state general fund budget, Proposition 111 also revised the formula for the minimum funding guarantee for public schools and community colleges.

As described above, Proposition 98 guaranteed, first, the "1986-87 percentage of revenues formula," giving schools and colleges collectively the same percentage of state general fund tax revenues as received in 1986-87. Also included is the second, now called "maintenance of effort," guarantee. This section assures to schools and colleges their prior year funding level, adjusted for increases in enrollment and changes in cost of living (COLA). Proposition 111 changed the cost-of-living basis in the "maintenance of effort" formula. Specifically, it requires that per capita personal income in California, rather than the lower U. S. Consumer Price Index, serve as the COLA to determine maintenance of effort.

The proposition also allows the state to reduce the minimum funding guarantee in a year of low revenue growth. However, should that provision be activated, the funding base must be restored in subsequent years so education eventually receives the amount that would have been allocated had no reduction occurred.

The impact of this measure depends upon its effect on the minimum funding guarantee and on excess revenues. Generally speaking, Proposition 111 tends to increase the minimum funding guarantee because it increases the cost-of-living element in the maintenance of effort formula. Thus, the maintenance of effort formula more often determines the amount of the guarantee. Of course, when the economy slows, as in 1991 to 1994, a suspension of Proposition 98 could override the advantages of the new COLA basis.

1996—SENATE BILL 1977: CLASS SIZE REDUCTION

With the downturn in California's economy during the late 1980s and early 1990s, schools received nothing, or very little, by way of a cost-of-living adjustment (COLA). As a result, districts balanced their budgets by increasing class size. The number of California students per teacher increased K-12 from average classes of 27.1 students per class in 1995 to 29.1 in 1997. The state had the second largest average classroom size in the U. S. until 1996-1997, when Governor Wilson and the California Legislature approved funds to lower class size in K-3 grades to a maximum of 20 students per teacher (Fellmeth & Weichel, 2001).

Within two years, class size in the primary grades approached the national average. However, classes in grades 4-12 continued to exceed the national average; EdSource estimated that in 1999-2000 California still remained 49th among the states in number of students per teacher (EdSource, 2001).

Early analysis of California's class size reduction is positive. In 1998, STAR results were examined for smaller, in comparison to larger, class size; significant gains were made by students in smaller classes. This finding was repeated in the 1999 data, with students in the second and third grades showing the greatest improvement of any grade level.

1997–SENATE BILL 376: STANDARDIZED TESTING AND REPORTING (STAR) PROGRAM

Under the leadership of Governor Pete Wilson, the Standardized Testing and Reporting (STAR) program was approved by the legislature in 1997. This legislation requires all California school districts to use a single standardized test to assess each student in grades two through eleven each year. The California Board of Education selected the Stanford Achievement Test, Ninth Edition (SAT9) as the test to be administered.

Students in grades two through eight must be tested in the basic skills of reading, spelling, writing, and math. Students in grades nine through eleven must be tested in reading, writing, math, history/social science, and science. The objective of the testing program is to provide California citizens, the legislature, and educators with an objective view of student achievement. Additional information regarding the testing program is included later in this chapter.

1998—PROPOSITION 227: BILINGUAL EDUCATION

The original objective of bilingual education was to ensure that students would not fall behind academically because of a poor command of English and that students would gradually be taught English as a second language. Those who favored this approach argued that if language-minority students were taught some subjects in their native tongue, they would learn English without sacrificing content knowledge.

Critics of this approach argued that the program would keep students in a cycle of native language dependency, thus inhibiting English language acquisition. Public sentiment against bilingual education, which had many forms, continued to increase, so that enough signatures were gathered to place an initiative on the ballot in June 1998. Proposition 227 was overwhelmingly approved and virtually eliminated California's bilingual program.

The terms of the proposition require that limited English proficient (LEP) students be placed in English immersion classes and then mainstreamed into regular classes. The proposition allowed parents to obtain a waiver under some circumstances to keep a student in a bilingual program. Despite the "English only" message of Proposition 227, the debate over how best to instruct linguistically diverse students is far from decided.

1998-2000—GOVERNOR DAVIS'S PLAN FOR EDUCATION

As the 20th century came to a close, two events occurred that had a significant impact on school finance in California. The first event was an upturn in California's economy. For the first time in a decade, the state had a surplus of money, and the governor and legislature were willing to provide schools with a substantial portion of the surplus.

The second event was the 1998 election of Gray Davis, a governor with a strong commitment to education. In his first State of the State address in January 1999, Davis made it clear that education would be his "first, second, and third priority" (Governor's Office, 1999). Under his leadership several educational initiatives were approved by the legislature. Highlights of those initiatives follow.

REDUCING CLASS SIZE. The governor continued to fund the class size reduction initiated by Governor Wilson and expanded the program by providing funds to reduce class size in the 9th grade as well. Districts could receive funds to reduce class size in one subject area or two, English being required, while the second subject might be math, science, or social science.

TEACHER PEER ASSISTANCE AND REVIEW PROGRAM (PAR). Governor Davis allocated $41 million as an incentive for districts to implement teacher peer assistance and review programs for veteran teachers. PAR requires teachers, administrators, districts, and unions to work together to assist veteran teachers in improving their instructional programs.

PUBLIC SCHOOL ACCOUNTABILITY ACT. In 1999 Governor Davis sponsored legislation that became known as the Public Schools Accountability Act. The legislation is designed to track and compare a school's performance over a period of time. In January of 2000 every California public school was given an index, a ranking, and a target for improvement. First, each school was assigned an Academic Performance Index (API) based on student achievement on the Stanford 9 examination. The API has a possible scale from 200 to 1000. The first scores were released in June of 2000; API scores ranged from 302 to 966, with 1000 being a perfect score. Each school scoring below 800 was assigned a growth target, which was 5% of the difference between its score and 800. For example, a school scoring 600 had a target of 610. A score of 800 was established as the ultimate goal for all California schools. Those schools scoring at 800 or above are required to maintain or improve their current score.

The API score continues to be used to rank schools on a statewide basis and in comparison to schools with similar characteristics. Every year, schools must show a 5% growth in API performance and demonstrate that the achievement of ethnic minorities and economically disadvantaged students has improved comparably to other students in the school. Part of the program includes financial awards to schools and individual teachers whose students show improvement on the API. Work is under way to expand the data that contribute to the API to include other academic measures.

HIGH SCHOOL PROFICIENCY EXAMINATION. In 1999 Governor Davis proposed, and the legislature approved, a mandatory high school exit examination. The examination looks at the academic areas of language arts and math. This test, which high school students will be required to pass beginning in 2004, is meant to certify that students have achieved the level of education California considers adequate for a high school diploma. The exam is intended to ensure that all California high school graduates possess the skills and knowledge needed to be successful in college or the workplace.

Students may try the test as freshmen, but must take it beginning in the sophomore year. If they do not pass, they are allowed to keep retaking those portions they have not passed. The test involves math questions, including first-year algebra, English questions, and two writing samples.

Twenty-two states now require students to take an examination to graduate from high school. In many states, a high percentage of students lack the necessary skills, especially in math, to pass the exam. In large measure, this failure is because students have not been taught the often rigorous material that is found on the exams. There is no accurate count of how many students have failed the tests nationally, but the number has been estimated in the tens of thousands since the exams were introduced in the 1980s ("Next spring," 2000). For example, Arizona had planned to require the class of 2001 to pass the exam, but revised the schedule to 2002 for reading and writing and postponed math until 2004. This revised schedule occurred when officials found that only 12% of the 2001 class had passed the exam as sophomores (Groves, 2000).

2000—PROPOSITION 38: SCHOOLS OF CHOICE (THE VOUCHER INITIATIVE)

The notion of allowing parents to choose a school for their children to attend was part of President George Bush's educational program and was supported by California Governor Pete Wilson. In 1992 proponents circulated an initiative entitled "Parent Choice" that would have required California to provide a scholarship or voucher for every school-age child in an amount equal to at least 50% of state and local funding for K-12 education.

The initiative, Proposition 174, received enough signatures to appear on the June 1994 ballot. However, Governor Wilson placed the initiative on the ballot for November 1993. The initiative was overwhelmingly defeated by nearly 70% of those who went to the polls. At that time, supporters of the voucher vowed to continue the fight for "schools of choice," announcing that another initiative could be expected in the future.

The future took seven years to arrive. Proposition 36, another voucher initiative, was placed on the November 2000 ballot. This proposition was sponsored by Tim Draper, a Silicon Valley millionaire. The proposition echoed Proposition 174 with the exception that the voucher would carry a value of $4,000, instead of the $2,600 offered in 1993. Draper hoped to avoid some of the criticism of Proposition 174 by writing in a requirement that a private school that accepted a voucher had to include academic testing.

The education community breathed a huge sigh of relief when the measure failed with a 71% "no" vote. Schools of choice was a campaign issue in the 2000 election between George W. Bush and Al Gore. Although Bush became president, time will tell whether the voucher movement is dead in California or if it will be revived for a third time.

2000—PROPOSITION 39: GENERAL OBLIGATION BONDS

Although local General Obligation (GO) Bond elections were eliminated by Proposition 13, they were reinstated in 1986 by passage of Proposition 46. This proposition was an important restoration of capital outlay funding ability to school districts. It also allowed school districts to form special districts to sell construction bonds, subject to 2/3 approval of the voters in the special district.

The catch for many California districts was the 2/3 requirement. Most districts discovered that in the face of strong local resistance, passage of a bond initiative was next to impossible. Over the last 22 years, fully 44% of all school bond proposals that won majority support fell short of the 2/3 required for passage. Almost 90% of the bond issues that failed would have passed without the two-thirds rule (Elias, 2000).

Consequently, the educational community attempted several times to change the requirement for passage of a GO Bond measure from 2/3 of the vote to a simple majority. California citizens voted on this change in majority requirement in 1993 and spring of 2000. Both measures failed. As a compromise measure, the educational community agreed to place Proposition 39 on the fall, 2000, ballot. This proposition, which passed by a narrow margin, lowered the required vote for passage of general obligation bonds from 2/3 to 55%. More details regarding bond issues and requirements are discussed in Chapter 15, the facilities chapter.

SUMMARY

California citizens expressed an early commitment to education. This commitment was formalized in California's first constitution with the requirement that each district provide for a public school. A major factor in the history of California's public education is the state's attempt to cope with the problems associated with increased student enrollment. This problem became particularly acute with the coming of World War II and continued through the end of the 20th century. Other legislation, initiatives, and programs designed by state leaders have shaped and molded California's public education.

The balance of this chapter offered a discussion of educational issues with a focus on school finance that came to the fore in the second half of the 20th century. Perhaps the most significant change in financing public education occurred in 1978 with the passage of Proposition 13, when a shift was made from local finance of education by property taxes to state financial support of education with a mix of state income tax, state sales tax, and property tax. This means of financing public education has continued into the 21st century. The chapter contained a discussion of other legislation, initiatives, and programs designed by state leaders that have shaped and molded California's public education.

KEY TERMS

Gann Limit
High School Proficiency Exam
Proposition 13
Proposition 38
Proposition 39
Proposition 98
Proposition 111
Proposition 227

Public School Accountability Program
Senate Bill 90
Senate Bill 813
Senate Bill 1977
Serrano v. Priest
STAR Program
Teacher Assistance and Review
    Program (PAR)

DISCUSSION/ESSAY QUESTIONS

1. The story of public education in California is largely dominated by the state attempting to cope with ever-increasing numbers of students. With hindsight, should the state have provided greater resources to local school districts to assist in the construction of schools? Justify your answer. If you believe greater resources should have been provided by the state, what would have been the source of the funds?

2. Discuss the pros and cons of the equal funding of California school districts that resulted from the *Serrano v. Priest* decision.

3. Give two arguments in favor of Proposition 13 and two opposing arguments.

4. Proposition 98 was promoted as extremely beneficial for California public education. Has this promise been fulfilled or not? Justify your answer.

5. Class size reduction has taken a sizeable chunk of the state's educational budget. Have the citizens of the state received the benefits of this expenditure or not? Justify your answer.

7. Proposition 227 virtually ended the state's bilingual education program. Give two persuasive and two opposing arguments for the proposition.

8. Briefly discuss three of Governor Davis' educational programs and include your evaluation of the effectiveness of the programs.

CHAPTER 3

CALIFORNIA EDUCATION:
CHALLENGES AND OPPORTUNITIES

INTRODUCTION

Government institutions, including the United States government, state governments, and school districts, are similar to private organizations in that each institution faces an array of challenges. Some challenges are long-standing and ongoing, while new ones occur every day. Leaders of an institution exert a powerful influence on the ways in which challenges are met. The will and desire of the people exert a powerful influence on the shape and control of the institution itself. Many factors, including an institution's financial condition, its organizational structure, and its economic and social conditions, affect its reactions to the challenges that confront it.

In the case of California, state leadership has a profound effect on education. The political ambitions of the governor and each legislator, his or her philosophy, judgement, and wisdom make an immense difference in the path the institution will take. The level of funding for schools, the curriculum and programs that are offered and required, and the types of training and certification required of teachers and other personnel are all influenced, if not determined, by state leadership.

A major factor in funding for a state's educational program is the wealth of that state. Are available tax dollars sufficient to build schools, employ teachers and staff, and provide essential instructional materials and facilities? Every state must grapple with providing resources for the many competing needs of its citizens: education, police and fire protection, health needs, adequate transportation, and so on.

Each state must make decisions about allocation of resources. In this process, education must compete with a multitude of demands. If a state does not have or is unwilling to allocate resources for education to cope with an increase in student enrollment, then per-pupil expenditures decline. A consequence of this financial decline may create difficulties in recruiting high caliber teachers and administrators. Other consequences may include an increase in class size, reduced funds for curriculum development, and inability to purchase essential books and instructional materials. Furthermore, school districts may have insufficient funds to maintain existing school facilities or to construct new school plants to accommodate increased student enrollment.

This chapter delineates some of the primary political, social, and economic challenges that influence the conditions of education in California. Among the many challenges with which California citizens must cope are the staggering numbers of students to be served, the diversity of the student body, the training and recruitment of qualified teachers, and the financial ability and desire of California citizens to support education. These factors have had measurable effects upon the quality of education provided for California students.

The primary financial and educational challenges that impact the California educational system include:

- control of California public schools

- the financial condition of the state and its people

- resources allocated for education

- increasing student and adult population

- the influx of minority students into the system

- academic achievement of California students

- the option of further class size reduction

- need for educational technology

- the direction and effect of virtual teaching/learning

- the growth and direction of the charter school movement

- need for adequate financing of special education

- public concern with student social promotion

- need for funds for school construction and maintenance

- the need to train and recruit California teachers

- the need to improve the health and welfare of California children.

CONTROL OF CALIFORNIA PUBLIC SCHOOLS

As noted in Chapter 2, the control of schools has largely shifted from local school boards to the governor and state legislature. Political scientists and policymakers have long been concerned about the consolidation of political power in Sacramento. Those who believe in local control have expressed anxiety, and often frustration, as decision-making has shifted from local governments to the state.

A major shift in financial control of school districts occurred with passage of Senate Bill 90 in 1972. This legislation established a formula for maximum per-pupil income for school districts and took away the authority of local school boards authority to increase taxes. For this formula, the state established the term "revenue limit."

State control was further expanded with the passage of Proposition 13 in June of 1978. This proposition amended the state constitution to restrict annual ad valorem taxes to 1% of a property's market value and limited the conditions under which property assessments could be increased. Proposition 13 gave local school boards very few revenue enhancement powers. Local voters are denied the opportunity to levy ad valorem taxes in excess of the 1% rate except when bonds are approved. Even this power was further limited by the requirement of a 2/3 vote until the year 2000, when Proposition 39 lowered the requirement to 55%.

FINANCIAL CONDITION OF THE STATE AND ITS PEOPLE

California has the largest and most diverse economy in the nation. In 1999 the state entered into its sixth consecutive year of expansion. California is a wealthy state, and its products are the most numerous among the 50 states. New York state ranks second, with an economy about 70% the size of California's. If California were a separate nation, it would rank sixth in the world, exceeded only by the U. S., Japan, Germany, the United Kingdom, and France (Hill, 2000).

California residents receive a higher average personal income per capita than residents in most other states. In 1997 California, with per capita personal income at $26,218 as compared with the national average of $25,298, ranked 14th in the nation. While the income is higher than that in most other states, the tax burden is also higher. California citizens in 1999 paid a higher percentage of taxes per $100 of income than in 41 other states (Hill, 2000). In 1999 Californians had the highest tax burden in the nation at $2,184, while Texas residents were paying $891 (U. S. Census, 2000).

AMOUNT SPENT FOR EDUCATION

Schools are big business; in fact, they are the third largest business in California, trailing only aerospace and agriculture in total annual expenditures. In the 1960s, California public schools were the envy of the country and the world. In 1978, California's funding of education was 20% above the national average. That year the state ranked 17th nationwide in per pupil expenditures. Education was among California's growth industries and one of its highest priorities. California's universities were consistently ranked at the very top in the nation and the world. California public schools had little to fear from parent or community dissatisfaction with public education.

California's expenditures per pupil, in comparison to the rest of the nation, began to decline in the late 1970s and early 1980s. Per-pupil spending had dropped to 26th among the states by 1983. In 1997-1998 California ranked 40th in funding of public education, with $34 of every $1,000 of personal income going toward public education expenditures, as compared with Michigan ($48), Texas and New Jersey ($45), and New York ($44). By 1999, the state's relative investment had declined to near the very bottom of the states; only West Virginia and several Southern states ranked lower. In that year California ranked 41st, spending approximately $5,600 while New Jersey was spending $10,427 per student. Texas, with the second highest enrollment in the nation, was spending approximately $600 more per pupil than California (Fellmeth & Weichel, 2000). California is approximately $1,000 below the national average in expenditures per student, and below all nine other industrial states (Ed-Data, 2000).

The problem is not lack of means. While California is above average in the taxes it collects from its citizens, it spends proportionately less of those tax revenues on K-12 schools than nearly all other states. Nationwide, it is estimated that 49% of all state and local tax receipts are allocated to support K-12 schools, but California spends only about 40% for this purpose (EdData, 2000). While the state ranks very low in per capita expenditure for education, it ranks much higher in several other categories; for example, fourth in expenditures for prison operations, fourth in police and fire protection, and 16th in public welfare (EdSource, 2001).

John Mockler, executive director to the California State Board of Education, who helped write the state's school funding law, provides a historical comparison of California's commitment to education. In 1972, he pointed out, California's spending on schools represented about 5.6% of the state's personal income. In 1997 the state spent about 3.7% of personal income on schools, representing a loss of $17 billion (Colvin & Lesher, 1997).

The monies available per pupil affect the number of students per classroom, the amount spent on teachers' salaries, and other items that directly alter the learning experiences of students. Another major result of limited school funding is that school districts and communities must deal with uncertainty, knowing that reductions are often necessary to balance the district budget.

INCREASE IN STATE POPULATION

A brief summary of California's population growth will assist the reader in understanding the state's ongoing challenge in providing for its citizens. In 1850, when statehood was achieved, the population was less than 100,000 citizens. By 1900 this figure had jumped to 1,485,053, and by 1940, to 6,907,387. In 1960, only 20 years later, the population had more than doubled to 15,717,204; it almost doubled again to 29,760,021 in 1990. There were 547,000 Californians added in 1998 and another 571,000 in 1999. By the time of the 2000 census, the population numbered 33,871,648 (U. S. Census, 2000). To put this increase in perspective, the yearly expansion of the state's population is roughly equal to the total combined population of San Bernardino and Sacramento or the entire state of Wyoming.

STUDENT POPULATION. Obviously, California's public school population reflects the growth in the state's general population. Figure 1 reflects trends in California public and private school enrollment from 1976 through 2000. Figure 2 provides additional information about trends and projections in California school enrollment (California Department of Education, 2000a).

Between 1989 and 1999, the number of students enrolled in K-12 schools increased by 23%. The California Department of Education predicts that this growth will continue at approximately 140,000 per year for the next eight years, already exceeding six million students in the year 2001-02 (California Department of Education, 2001).

Class size reduction also significantly adds to the problem of providing adequate space. Districts are constantly examining options for housing new students, including leasing or purchasing portable classrooms, rehabilitation of existing facilities, establishing year-round schedules, double sessions, and extended days.

California's public school population is the largest in the nation. One of every eight U. S. students, kindergarten through grade 12, is educated in California's public schools, and projections indicate that enrollment will continue to increase. To educate California's student population, California employs approximately 284,000 teachers and operates more than 8,300 public schools in approximately 1,000 school districts.

Figure 1

California School Enrollment

Public and Private, 1976-2000

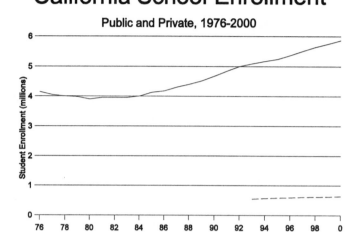

Note: Figures do not include students in ungraded programs.

Figure 2

Public School Enrollment

Trends and Projections 1976-2009

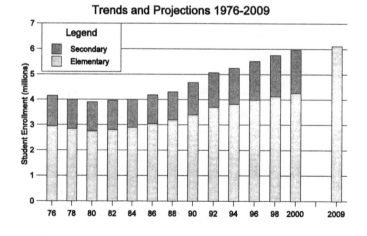

Note: Figure for 2009 is a K-12 estimate.
SOURCE: California Department of Education, 2000

INCREASE OF MINORITY STUDENTS. A major challenge and opportunity for California educators is the ethnic and linguistic diversity of students enrolled in the public schools. The California State Department of Education (2000) projects that school enrollment will continue to diversify. For example, between 1997 and 2007, the number of white students is expected to decline by 16%, while the Hispanic student population will increase by 35%, Pacific Islander by 30%, and Asian by 15% (see Figures 3 and 4).

Associated with ethnic diversity is the variety of language backgrounds in the state. California students have as their primary language more than 55 languages and dialects. In 1997 English learners (ELs) made up nearly 25% of the student population and comprised more than 33% of the students in primary grades (EdSource, 2001). In the Los Angeles Unified School District nearly 280,000 limited-English-speaking students represent some 40% of enrollment. The number of limited-English-speaking students is projected to increase continually in the foreseeable future. Although this enrollment is increasing statewide, the major growth is found in seven southern and Central Valley counties: San Bernardino, Riverside, Los Angeles, San Diego, San Joaquin, Fresno, and Sacramento.

As a result of this influx of students whose primary language is other than English, a major challenge is to find the best ways to teach these young people and adequate resources to provide them with primary language support, develop English fluency, and prepare them for the daily demands of an unfamiliar environment.

STUDENT ACHIEVEMENT

California students rank below the national average in basic skills achievement. According to the 1998 National Assessment of Educational Progress in reading, only 20% of California fourth-grade students and 22% of eighth-graders were proficient readers. The fourth-graders ranked 29th among the 39 states in which students were tested. Eighth-grade students ranked 26th out of 36 states. Math achievement, tested in 2000, was even lower, with only 18% of California eighth-graders scoring proficient or above, a score that placed California 27th among the 39 participating states (National Center for Education Statistics, 2001).

Since 1998 California has used the Stanford-9 achievement test for its Standardized Testing and Reporting (STAR) program. The test measures basic academic skills of students, including English learners, enrolled in grades 2 through 11. Initial statewide test results were disappointing. However, improvement has been demonstrated each year by all subgroups: racial/ethnic, socioeconomic, and English proficient (CalFacts, 2000). By spring of 2001 average scores fell at or above the 50th national percentile in math and language through grade 9. Only grades 10 and 11 in those subjects and grades 3 through 11 in reading

Figure 3

Growth in Minority Enrollment

as Percent of Total 1971 - 2001

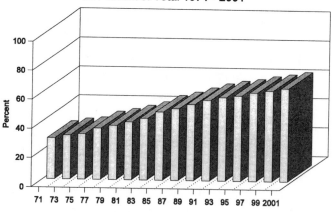

Note: Figure for 2001 is an estimate.

Figure 4

Change in Ethnic Distribution

as Percent of K-12 Enrollment 1971 - 2000

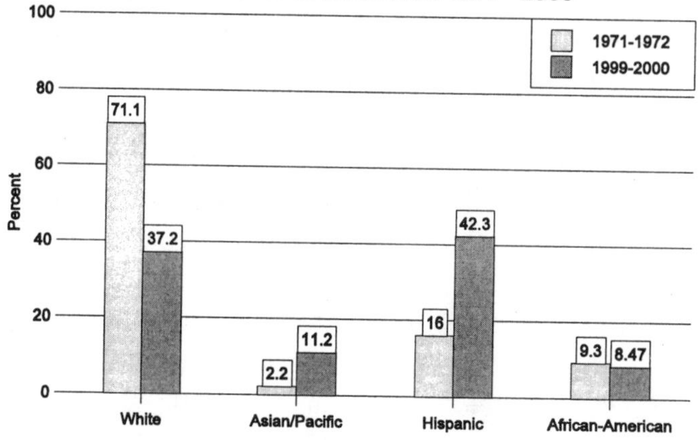

SOURCE: California Department of Education, 2001

had not yet reached that target (California Department of Education, 2001). As of the year 2001, the STAR program did not yet reflect all of the state academic content standards. Educators are hopeful that continued academic progress will be demonstrated when alignment is complete.

CLASS SIZE

The number of California students per teacher increased from the 1987-1988 year to record highs in the mid-1990s. The state had the second largest average classroom size in the U. S. until 1996-1997, when the legislature budgeted and Governor Wilson approved an infusion of funds to lower class size to 20 students in kindergarten through third grades. However, class size at grades 4 through 12 continues to remain high, with an estimate that California still ranks 49th among the 50 states, at 4.8 more students per class than the national average (EdSource, 2001).

A major challenge for educators is to verify objectively that class size reduction actually results in improved student achievement. If class size reduction does achieve the objective of improving student performance, the next goal for the citizens of the state must be to provide the resources to carry class size reduction through all grades.

TECHNOLOGY

At first glance, one might assume that California schools lead the nation in the utilization of technology in the classroom. This assumption would probably be based on California's reputation as a national leader in the development of technology and its concentration of high-tech companies. Nevertheless, the assumption is false, according to EdSource (1998b).

In 1996 California ranked 45th of the 50 states, with 14 students for every computer, compared to the national rate of 10. A 1998 survey moved California from 45th to 47th. In 1999 California had moved to 8.1 students per computer, but the rest of the nation had moved faster, and the state remained last (*Education Week*, 1999).

Then, action was taken to address this area of need. The governor's 2000 budget contained $175 million for one-time acquisition of computers for K-12 schools. Another $25 million was included to train K-12 teachers to effectively use computers and other technology in the classroom.

VIRTUAL TEACHING/LEARNING

Perhaps the most revolutionary change in education since the invention of printing is the Internet. Will school campuses, textbooks, and teachers who are assigned a classroom of students disappear within the next few years? Sounds farfetched, but perhaps not. Some $6 billion in venture capital has been invested in the education sector since 1990. The president of Cisco Systems has referred to education as "the next big killer application on the Internet" (Grimes, 2000).

Universities and trade schools have taken the lead in virtual learning, but K-12 schools are soon to follow. The University of Phoenix Online claims a virtual student body of 60,000. In elementary and secondary education, home schooling and charter schools have taken the lead; students complete their education with little direct face-to-face contact with a teacher. All the lessons, all the homework, and all the examinations are completed online.

The education community received surprising news in December of 2000 when William Bennett, former U. S. Secretary of Education, announced that he was opening a for-profit cyberspace K-12 school that would offer a complete elementary and secondary education. The surprise lay in the fact that Bennett had previously expressed concern about cyber teaching; he had written, "Keep one thing in mind: so far, there is no good evidence that most uses of computers significantly improve learning" (Helfland, 2000b). Helfand attributes the quote to Bennett's book, *The Educated Child*.

The school opened grades K-2 in September 2001 under the name K12 Inc., with plans to extend the program through high school. Initially, tuition for a full program was about $1,000 annually, with additional services to be added at additional cost. Financial analysts estimate that the market for cyber-based education is lucrative, worth billions of dollars (Helfand, 2000b).

The research and arguments, both pro and con, as to the educational value of learning online will continue unabated for some time, but thoughts of no school construction, no school buses, no textbooks, no school lunches, and no school principals will be powerful financial stimuli to make such programs work.

CHARTER SCHOOLS

Senator Gary Hart was successful in managing passage of SB 1448 (1992), which initially allowed up to 100 schools to be identified as charter schools. These charter schools are governed by their charter petitions, but are otherwise exempt from all state laws regulating education, except for those that relate to the State Teachers' Retirement System. The 1992 law was amended in 1998 to permit 250 additional charters in that year and 100 additional charters in each subsequent year.

Any individual may petition a school board for permission to form a school as long as 10% of the teachers in a district or 50% of the teachers in a school agree. An appeal process is included in the event a school board declines to approve a charter.

State funding is to go directly to the charter school in an amount matching the base revenue limit of the district. The school may apply for categorical aid. Tuition may not be charged, and the school may not set admission requirements that violate standards against discrimination or sectarianism. The intent of the charter school legislation is to facilitate parent choice and more rapid innovation within the public education system. The expectation is that if educators are freed from regulation by the district and the state, quality will improve. The legislation is revolutionary in terms of the freedom from state laws and regulations that has been granted to those schools.

California legislation requires the Legislative Analyst to complete an evaluation of the charter school movement by July 1, 2003. The evaluation must include the effectiveness of the charter schools and a recommendation for expansion or reduction of the permitted annual growth of charter schools.

SPECIAL EDUCATION

About 10% of the total student enrollment in California qualifies for special education, and the proportion is growing. The cost of special education is borne jointly by the federal and state government. The U. S. Congress promised in 1975 to pay 40% of the cost of educating children with disabilities, but it has never allocated funds to cover more than 13% of the cost (Helfand, 2000a).

Paul Goldfinger, vice-president of a school finance consulting firm, estimates that the federal government would need to contribute an additional one billion dollars per year to meet its 40% obligation (Goldfinger, 2001). This unfilled promise has forced districts to take funds from the general fund to support special education. Consequently, school boards and superintendents complain that they cannot meet the needs of special education students without shortchanging students in regular education.

The California education community received good news in the fall of 2000 when the state of California settled a 20-year fight to increase funds for special education. The special education dispute began in 1980, when the Riverside County Office of Education sued the state, alleging that its districts were being forced to pay for services for special education students that exceeded federal requirements. Under the settlement, the state will pay $520 million to reimburse school districts and counties for past costs relating to special education. The state will also add an additional $100 million each year to the current allocation for special education ("Agreement ends," 2000).

AB 1626—SOCIAL PROMOTION

In 1998, the California Legislature, at the urging of Governor Pete Wilson, passed legislation designed to eliminate "social promotion." Social promotion is defined as passing a student from one grade to the next when the student has not mastered the basic skills required for advancement to the next grade.

The legislation required all California school districts to adopt a policy for retention and promotion based on the results of the Stanford 9 norm-referenced achievement test. Districts also have the option of using indicators of academic achievement designated by the district. Students in grades one, four, seven, and ten who are not performing at grade level are required to take remedial classes in language arts, math, science, and history. Governor Wilson proclaimed, "If students are not up to the standard after taking their classes, they don't advance to the next grade" (ACSA, 1998).

Eliminating social promotion has become a popular political issue, with Texas, Delaware, South Carolina, and Wisconsin joining California in passing legislation to end the educational practice. For example, Texas requires students in grades three, five, and eight to pass tests in reading and math before they can be promoted to the next grade.

This trend is not supported by research. A 1989 analysis of 63 empirical studies by Holmes found that 54 of the studies showed that retention does more harm than good (Kelley, 1999). Yet the problem is severe. Dr. Robert Barner, head of intervention services for Los Angeles Unified School District, estimated that between 55% and 60% of Los Angeles students were not meeting the district standards for promotion (Barner, 1999).

The key to eliminating social promotion is early identification of students who are not making satisfactory progress followed by appropriate and successful remedial work (Kelly, 1999). Time will tell whether the California Legislature and the educational establishment will provide the necessary resources and programs to eliminate both social promotion and widespread retention.

FACILITIES

The need for new facilities results from both increases in student enrollment and the increasing number of older school buildings that are in need of repair, renovation, and modernization. The citizens of California spent more than $20 billion on school facilities from 1986 to 1996 (EdData, 2000). Even with this sizeable expenditure, thousands of California students are housed in temporary classrooms and attend schools desperately in need of maintenance and repair.

Districts are constantly examining options to meet facility needs, including portable classrooms, rehabilitation of existing facilities, year-round schedules, double sessions, and extended days. The passage of Proposition 39, which reduces the voter requirement from 2/3 to 55% for local bond approval to finance the acquisition of land and facilities, may go a long way to alleviate the facility problem.

TEACHER TRAINING AND RECRUITMENT

Increased student enrollment and reduced class size have dramatically increased the demand for teachers. Thus, the training and employment of an adequate number of teachers to fill California's rapidly growing number of classrooms continue to be among the state's most pressing problems.

California has a critical shortage of fully trained and credentialed teachers. By 1998 almost 30,000 California teachers, or nearly 10% of the state's teaching force, were employed with emergency credentials (EdSource, 2000). The situation is particularly acute in the academic areas of math and science, where potential teachers readily make more money in the private sector.

Elizabeth Hill, California's Budget Analyst, predicts that the state will need to hire nearly 300,000 new teachers over the next decade. Hill (2000) estimates that about 1/3 of the teachers in classrooms today will retire in the next ten years.

Research clearly demonstrates that teacher quality is one of the most important factors in student achievement. California's Governor Davis, with concurrence of the state legislature, provided several incentives in the 2000 budget to recruit and retain California teachers. The primary incentives include these provisions:

- **Governor's Teaching Fellowships**—$20 million in teaching fellowships were provided for 1,000 candidates. Teacher candidates will receive an award of $20,000 to help pay living and educational expenses while completing their teacher training programs. The successful candidates must make a four-year commitment to teach in a hard-to-staff school.

- **Teacher Hiring Incentives**—Each district will receive $2,000 for every credentialed teacher hired to replace an emergency permit teacher. An additional $2,000 will be awarded to each fully credentialed teacher hired to teach.

- **National Board Certification**—Teachers who are nationally board certified are already eligible for a $10,000 bonus. If the teacher agrees to teach in a low-performing school for a minimum of four years, he will be eligible for an additional $20,000 bonus. National certification is a rigorous process, requiring an   assessment of the teacher's competency in subject matter knowledge, teaching skills, school leadership, and community participation.

- **Teacher Housing Incentives**—Up to $10,000 in loans for the down payment on a home will be granted to 5,000 fully credentialed teachers. These loans are forgivable if the teacher agrees to serve for five years in a hard-to-staff school.

- **Teacher Recruitment Campaign**—The 2000 budget provided $9.4 million to establish five teacher recruitment centers in regions with the highest concentrations of emergency permit holders: Los Angeles, the Inland Empire, and the Central Valley. These centers will develop and implement aggressive recruitment strategies.

- **Teacher Internships**—Internship programs allow individuals pursuing teaching as a second career to complete their teacher preparation while serving as classroom teachers. School districts and universities jointly provide training and support to these interns.

- **Loan Forgiveness**—The loan forgiveness program provides up to $11,000 over four years for teachers in critical subject matter shortage areas, schools in low-income areas, and rural schools.

CONDITIONS OF CALIFORNIA CHILDREN

The Children's Advocacy Institute has published the California Children's Budget annually since 1993. As the name implies, the Advocacy Institute has an objective of improving life for California children. The budget published by the institute provides an alternative to the governor's proposed budget each year, along with recommendations for improving the conditions of children. The institute's publication provides facts regarding the conditions of California children. The highlights of the findings are presented for information and reflection by California citizens (Fellmeth, 2000).

- **Poverty**—In 2000-01, 2.6 million California children lived in poverty, defined as $16,450 or less annual income for a family of four. Over a quarter (28.6%) of children under the age of five were included in this group. California ranked 45th among the states and District of Columbia in poverty among children and youth.

  Enrollment in free or reduced-price meal programs indicated that approximately 2.7 million (47%) of the state's students came from low-income backgrounds. This concentration of children in need was surpassed only by Louisiana, Mississippi, and the District of Columbia. These children tend to be members of a minority group and relatively recent immigrants whose primary language is not English.

- **Health Coverage**—It was estimated in 1999-2000 that 18% of California children were without health insurance. One-third of the state's uninsured children were under six years of age. California ranks 46th among the states and District of Columbia in insurance coverage for children and youth.

- **Unwed Parents**—Poverty is driven most critically by unwed births. More than 32% of infants in California are born to unwed mothers, including more than 60% of African-American births and 40% of Hispanic births. Single-parent families have median household incomes only 20% to 25% that of two-parent households.

- **Hunger**—A 1996 national survey of hunger found that California ranks 49th among the 50 states in alleviating hunger among children under the age of twelve. Only Louisiana had a higher percentage of undernourished children.

- **Child Abuse**—In 1997, 480,443 child abuse reports were classified as requiring "emergency responses." This number was up from 396,100 in 1995. The rate of increase in the number of reported cases in California was second highest in the nation.

- **High School Completion**—The state ranks 46th in the percentage of 18- to 24-year-olds who complete high school.

- **Crime**—California's prison population increased from 19,000 in 1977 to more than 260,000 in 1999. Incarceration of each prisoner involves approximately $22,000 in direct costs and close to $40,000 per year with capital costs included. Juvenile incarceration is estimated at $41,000 per person per year. The state ranks sixth among the fifty states in the commission of juvenile violent crime and 48th of the 50 states and District of Columbia in juvenile incarceration (Hill, 2000).

Summary

The residents of California face formidable educational challenges during this decade. Most educators and citizens are in agreement that the greatest challenge is to improve student achievement, achievement that will prepare students for responsible citizenship, success in college and the world of work, and a productive life. While there is little argument about the importance of improved student achievement, opinion is not unanimous regarding how to achieve the goal or how to finance it. Among the challenges are limits on the amount of tax dollars allocated to education; means of coping with increased enrollment; the particular needs of minority students, especially English learners; and the needs of children born into poverty. Other issues include the need for new facilities, the direction and effect of virtual teaching and learning, and the training and recruitment of teachers.

KEY TERMS

Budget for education
Child abuse
Children's Advocacy Institute
Crime
Facilities
Governor's Teaching Fellowships
Health coverage
High school completion
Hunger
Increase of minority students
National Board Certification

Per capita personal income
Per pupil expenditure
Social promotion
State Legislature
Student achievement
Teacher training and recruitment
Teacher hiring incentives
Teacher housing incentives
Teacher internships
Technology
Unwed parents

DISCUSSION/ESSAY QUESTIONS

1. In 1978 California ranked 17th nationwide in per-pupil expenditures for education. By 1999-2000 this ranking was near the lowest of all the states. Discuss three major reasons for this decline in California's ranking.

2. While California ranks near the bottom of the states in total tax receipts spent on education, it ranks much higher in per capita expenditures for public health, police protection, and public welfare. Discuss three major reasons for this disparity.

3. California has an increasing percentage of students representing ethnic and racial minorities. What implications does this fact have for California school finance?

4. During the past decade, the number of California children living in poverty has shown a dramatic increase. Discuss the major factors contributing to this increase and the financial implications for California school districts.

5. California politicians are banking on class size reduction as a means of improving students' academic performance. Do you expect their hopes to be realized? Support your answer by citing appropriate research studies.

CHAPTER 4

ROLE OF THE CHIEF BUSINESS OFFICER

INTRODUCTION

California schools are big business. The annual expenditure for K-12 education in 2000-01 was more than $28 billion, or approximately 40% of California tax revenues. These funds were distributed to 988 districts and 58 counties. In many communities the school district is the major industry, with the largest number of employees and the highest payroll.

California has three types of public school districts: elementary, secondary, and unified. Elementary districts may contain grades K-6 or K-8; secondary districts include grades 7-12 or 9-12; and unified districts contain all grades from K through 12. There were approximately 1,000 districts in California in July of 2000. The number of districts changes as districts unify or as a district divides to form two or more separate districts. For example, dividing the Los Angeles Unified School District into several smaller districts has been discussed for many years.

Of California districts, 45% have less than 1,000 students. Approximately 40% of the districts number 1,000 to 10,000. Districts that include 10,000 to 50,000 students represent 13% of the total. Only eight districts have more than 50,000 students, with Los Angeles topping the list at 600,000 (*California Public School Directory*, 2000).

This chapter discusses the person responsible for the day-to-day management of this significant commitment of California taxpayers. As the previous sections of this text indicate, the pressure on school boards, superintendents, and staff has increased significantly as a result of the "squeeze" on financial resources for California schools. The complexities of school accounting, major legislation, and ballot initiatives also account for major stress on districts and their leadership. All but the smallest districts employ a chief business official (CBO) to manage the district's financial resources. In districts with very few employees, financial management may be the responsibility of the superintendent. The superintendent, in this case, is usually assisted in financial matters by a private consultant or a consultant from the county schools office. As enrollment increases warrant additional staff, first priority is usually placed on employing a business official. This need typically takes precedence over hiring a staff member to manage personnel or instruction.

TITLE AND PREPARATION

There is little consistency in titles of chief business officials in California school districts. The CBO may be designated the assistant superintendent of business, business manager, director of business, associate superintendent of business, or director of fiscal services. This variety of titles is due, in part, to a lack of certification requirements for the CBO. While the personnel officer and head of instruction require California teaching and administrative credentials, no credential is necessary for the head of the business department.

Business officials also bring to their assignments a wide variety of experience and training. Although a number of school business officials do have teaching and administrative backgrounds, many also lack such formal experience and training. A substantial number of business leaders possess training in business and accounting; a majority hold a college or university degree. However, a significant number do *not* have a college or university degree and gain their positions through experience. Many CBOs have been promoted after gaining experience in the business department as a payroll or purchasing clerk or in an accounting position.

There is a major difference between the work of a school business manager and a business official in private enterprise. In the private sector the business manager is concerned with a profit margin and is judged by how effectively that objective is achieved. The school business manager's objective is less well defined. The product of a school system, its students, is not as easily measured or evaluated as the profit in a business ledger. Perhaps that explains, in part, why school business officials find that they do not receive the same respect or financial remuneration as their counterparts in the private sector.

A comprehensive study of the characteristics of California CBOs was completed by the California Department of Education in 1989. The study found that the majority of CBOs are males (665), white, 45 to 50 years of age, expecting to retire within ten years. The annual salary of a CBO in 1999 was approximately $65,000. However, CBO salaries have increased significantly in recent years, now approaching $100,000 per year in many southern California school districts.

The study also found that a majority of CBOs were classified, rather than certificated, employees. A majority were college graduates, averaging 18 years' employment in school districts (Malone, 1998).

A major analysis of expectations for CBOs was completed by Terry Bustillos (1989) as part of a dissertation study. Dr. Bustillos solicited the opinions of governing board presidents, superintendents, and CBOs in ten southern California counties regarding their expectations of California business officials. He found a high level of agreement that the

CBO should have expertise in accounting, economics, and public administration. He also found a strong consensus on need for a practical understanding of all aspects of school business operations and collective bargaining.

DUTIES AND RESPONSIBILITIES

The role of the school business manager has changed significantly over the years, from that of bookkeeper to the increasingly complex and technical responsibility of accounting for the many programs offered by a school district. Job descriptions place the district's financial officer in a support role, rather than a line position. The business department exists to provide assistance to administrators and teachers with direct responsibility for education of students.

Both a review of the literature and an examination of sample CBO job descriptions reveal similarities in duties and responsibilities required of the CBO in various settings. The first responsibility of the position is providing resources for an efficient and effective educational program, a staff role.

However, the CBO has direct line—or supervisory—responsibility for the business office, maintenance and operations, transportation, and food services. Tasks under the direction of the CBO include financial planning and budgeting; fiscal accounting, reports, and auditing; payroll; purchasing and warehouse; insurance and risk management; facilities management; and providing fiscal information to the board of education, superintendent, and site administrators. Each of these areas of responsibility is discussed below.

STRATEGIC PLANNING. With school finance changing each year, many administrators feel that long-range financial plans are almost impossible. Nevertheless, successful districts develop long-range plans, commonly referred to as strategic plans. What are the financial objectives for the district and what are the strategies for achieving these objectives? Obviously, with a school district dependent on so many outside sources for revenue, strategic planning is not an easy task.

The effective strategic plan must include several assumptions and scenarios. For example, the state Lottery Commission projected an income of approximately $160 per pupil for 1990-1991, then subsequently revised that estimate to $127.

A second example of the need for strategic planning was a tripling of electricity costs in California in the 2000-2001 school year. CBOs began a frantic search for funds to pay the utilities, since that account had been underbudgeted in the budget just adopted. A good strategic plan would have included the possibility of reduced lottery funds or increased utility bills and would have maintained a reserve for such contingencies.

Many sources of information must contribute to a strategic plan. In addition to the usual enrollment projections and data from the county and state, the business manager should subscribe to one of several legislative updates. The CBO should also observe the economy closely by reading daily newspapers such as the *Wall Street Journal,* the *Los Angeles Times*, and the *San Francisco Chronicle.* Several CBOs subscribe to *Barron's* and *Forbes* magazines for the same reason. In addition to business reports, a number of professional journals in education should be "must" reading; valuable resources include the *California School Business Official Journal, Phi Delta Kappan,* and *Educational Leadership.*

To affect an organization, a strategic plan must be widely disseminated to the staff and community. If the plan includes something like refurbishing a gymnasium every five years at a cost in excess of half a million dollars, the community can be encouraged to develop a mind-set that recognizes this need. All successful plans should include a source of funds for the project. If refurbishing the gym includes a community election to pass an assessment tax, one must plan early to gain support for the project.

The most important objective of planning is to enable decision-makers to focus on the big picture, or long-range needs, and not just to react from one crisis to the next. Developing and effectively communicating a strategic plan for a district is probably one of the greatest challenges to the business manager.

FINANCIAL PLANNING AND BUDGETING. The district's CBO has a major responsibility for taking the district's goals, ensuring that they are student-centered, and calculating the dollars needed to accomplish those goals (White, 1997). The annual budget is one of the most important documents in any district. It is a blueprint of the district's priorities for that year. The budget should be based on sound objectives and contain well-supported assumptions for projected income and expenditures. As a financial plan that details a district's objectives, the budget should be developed and written to communicate those objectives to staff and citizens of the community.

Financial planning properly considers district needs several years into the future. These needs include the instructional program, facilities, maintenance and operations, and all other aspects of an effective program for students. The plans should be translated into revenue projections and expenditures, yet remain flexible as district needs change.

INFORMATION TECHNOLOGY. A major change in the role of the CBO occurred with the advent of information technology. The computer age started after World War II, but did not impact school financial operations until the mid-50s. The first use was to prepare payroll and accounting records. By 1965 mainframe computers were utilized by county offices and larger school districts. By 1975 personal computers started appearing in districts, and by 1985 most middle-size to larger districts were using personal computers in district offices, at school sites, and in some classrooms. By 1995 the majority of districts had developed some network-based systems, and at the turn of the century most districts had installed connections to the Internet (Malone, 1998).

Today a major portion of a CBO's daily work is done on a computer. Prior to the computer age, a district's financial reports were often complex and too detailed for management and board use. The computer has made it possible to prepare simplified financial information by utilizing graphs, charts, and spreadsheets. The amount of data generated in the future will make it even more important for the CBO to be effective in analyzing, preparing, and presenting data.

COLLECTIVE BARGAINING. Collective bargaining has become a major responsibility of CBOs in the past 25 years. The vast majority of California school district employees are members of a labor union. These unions have been most effective in lobbying for school resources. For example, the California Teachers Association was primarily responsible for the passage of Proposition 98, which provided school districts a minimum fixed amount of the state budget each year. Employee organizations carry clout with state legislators and the governor. Members of teacher and classified organizations often play a significant role in the election of local school board members.

Obviously, working with employee associations significantly influences the work of the CBO. Labor relations is a very time-consuming task, and the CBO's preparation of accurate information and the presentation of that information in credible fashion is critical in the collective bargaining process.

FISCAL ACCOUNTING, REPORTS, AND AUDITING. This set of tasks has become increasingly complex. Many CBOs would argue that the task is extremely burdensome, involving many reports required by county, state, and federal agencies. Although most districts have business staff to handle day-to-day accounting procedures, the CBO has final responsibility to ensure that all accounts and funds are properly documented and balanced. The successful CBO regularly presents to the superintendent and school board a status report on the district's financial condition.

As discussed in a later section of this text, California requires school districts to have all accounts and funds audited on a yearly basis by an independent auditor. The county superintendent of schools is also charged with monitoring school district finances.

PAYROLL. In most California school districts, funds for salaries and benefits constitute a major portion of the budget. Indeed, in many districts approximately 80% of the budget is allocated to this area. Therefore, the CBO has a major obligation to establish effective payroll procedures to account for every expenditure in this budget category. Careful attention should be devoted to monitoring overtime, substitute hours, and temporary hires, as expenditures in these categories may gradually accumulate to significant amounts.

The CBO should be directly involved in the collective bargaining process and project the ongoing cost of salary increases and related expenditures. Fringe benefits, a budget item whose cost has accelerated significantly in the past several years, exemplifies a major concern relative to payroll.

PURCHASING AND WAREHOUSE. The two major objectives of purchasing operations are to acquire supplies and equipment of the right quantity and quality and to obtain them at the lowest possible cost. To protect tax dollars, the legislature has enacted numerous rules and procedures to govern purchasing. As educational dollars decrease, the purchasing staff needs to go beyond legal requirements to provide instructional supplies for classrooms in adequate quantities and in timely fashion.

Careful analysis should be made of the advantages and disadvantages of establishing a district warehouse. Small districts may not find a warehouse cost-effective. As a rule of thumb, a warehouse becomes cost-effective when district enrollment approaches 5,000 students. However, this number is only a guideline, since particular circumstances, such as proximity to a major supplier or distances between schools, may influence the decision. Efficiency and cost control are the two key concepts in warehousing supplies and materials. Data processing equipment has enabled many districts to improve control over this business operation. Many districts are also using the Internet as a tool in the purchasing process.

INSURANCE AND RISK MANAGEMENT. As with many other aspects of business management, providing adequate and affordable insurance has become so complex as to require special training. Millions of taxpayer dollars are spent each year on insurance of various kinds. It is important that carefully conceived management practices be established in this area. Many California districts have united in joint powers agreements or other cooperative arrangements to provide adequate insurance coverage.

Risk management is concerned with providing a safe environment to protect students and staff from injury. Over the last several years many districts have designated their CBO as the safety officer. In this role, the CBO establishes training programs on safety for students and staff. Theoretically, proper education, management, and control would eliminate all risks and hazards, but it is questionable whether any district can ever reach that condition. Nevertheless, a well planned and managed safety program reduces injuries and losses.

FACILITIES MANAGEMENT. There are three issues in facilities management: new construction, maintaining facilities, and use of facilities. Each of these involves numerous laws, regulations, and procedures. A section later in this text is devoted to maintenance of facilities and construction of new facilities.

Criteria for use of facilities should be carefully outlined in district board policies and administrative procedures. Citizens of a community have paid for school facilities with tax dollars and are entitled to use them appropriately. By making adequate provision for access to school grounds, playfields, and classrooms, a district engenders strong community support for funds to maintain sites and to construct new schools.

MAINTENANCE AND OPERATIONS. A later section is devoted to this subject, but it is mentioned here as a responsibility assigned to most CBOs. The concept of "management by walking around" (MBWA) has become very popular in the last few years and perhaps should be a requirement in the job description of the CBO. Management by "walking on water" has also been suggested, but is difficult to implement! Regular visitations to school sites assist a CBO in identifying problems and create a basis for praising jobs well done—a most persuasive morale booster.

TRANSPORTATION. A section on this topic also appears later in the text. The CBO, even in the smallest California school district, needs expert assistance in managing this department. Such assistance may come from a lead bus driver or shop assistant in a small district, from a transportation director in a large district. This department often employs a large staff and represents a substantial capital investment.

The successful CBO periodically seeks services from outside the district to review the performance of the transportation department. Such an independent audit helps ensure safe and efficient transportation of students and a cost-effective operation.

FOOD SERVICES. Like transportation, food service is a support for students that usually falls under the aegis of the district's CBO. It, too, is a department highly regulated by state and federal legislation and other outside agencies. For example, county offices of education are responsible for ensuring that proper health standards are maintained in a district's kitchens and food service areas.

Many California districts contract with private business or with larger districts to provide this service. Each district has the primary duty of providing a nutritious meal for students at the lowest possible cost. Consultants from the county superintendent's office and the California Department of Education should be asked to complete a periodic review of the department to ensure that these objectives are being accomplished.

BOARD OF EDUCATION, SUPERINTENDENT, AND PRINCIPALS. The CBO, by training and experience, is uniquely qualified to keep the board, superintendent, and principals informed of the financial condition of the district. It is the CBO's task to warn of the financial consequences of a "great instructional idea" that the district may be unable to afford.

It also falls on the shoulders of the CBO to play the "black hat" role in salary negotiations. The CBO is charged to analyze the effect of a cost-of-living increase on the current and long-term condition of the budget. He or she should clearly and, if necessary, forcefully inform all members of the board's negotiating team, the superintendent, and the board of education as to financial consequences of a proposed agreement. Better yet to work closely with all groups to keep them apprised of the financial situation of the district as it changes. In this way, a more collaborative style of management may be utilized.

A successful CBO should be a leading member of a superintendent's cabinet. The CBO keeps the superintendent and school board informed of all business matters. This is a major responsibility that requires expert knowledge of finance, legal requirements, and the myriad rules and regulations imposed on California school districts. The CBO must constantly remain aware of the changing financial scene, particularly of all relevant legislation under consideration in Sacramento.

SUMMARY

California chief business officials are "key players" in the successful management of a school district. The responsibility of the CBO is exceeded only by that of the superintendent. In many districts, the superintendent is dependent on the CBO in most financial matters.

The areas of responsibility of the CBO are numerous and complex. They range from maintaining the solvency of the district to managing the food services program. Expert planning and organizational abilities are "musts" for this important position. Every district has a major responsibility to employ a highly capable CBO who has the ability and skill to manage the district's resources competently and effectively.

KEY TERMS

Assistant Superintendent of Business	MBWA
Budgeting	Payroll
Business Manager	Purchasing
CBO	Risk management
Director of Business	Safety Officer
District warehouse	Strategic planning
Financial planning	

DISCUSSION/ESSAY QUESTIONS

1. Typically, in a small district the first assistant to the superintendent to be employed is a business manager. Discuss the major reasons for this decision.

2. California does not require a teaching or administrative credential for service as a business manager. Is this a good or poor decision and why?

3. Responsibilities of the business manager have increased significantly in the past decade. Discuss three new tasks that have contributed to this increase in responsibilities.

4. Strategic planning is a major responsibility of the business manager. Discuss three major financial components that should be included in a district's strategic financial plan.

5. Some districts include the business manager as part of the district collective bargaining and negotiating team. Discuss the advantages and disadvantages of this practice.

CHAPTER 5

DEVELOPING THE BUDGET

INTRODUCTION

The state of California and all school districts are required to adopt a balanced budget each year. This chapter deals with the budgeting process. It concerns the role of the chief business officer in the process as well as legal budget guidelines, the work of the school financial resources committee, and estimating the succeeding year's income and expenses.

The school district budgeting process involves continuous planning and evaluation. A basic assumption for every district or school is that the budget is a spending *plan*—a plan to accomplish the instructional objectives of the district. A budget is never etched in stone, but typically is modified several times during the fiscal year. A second assumption for school boards, superintendents, and principals is that the solvency of the district must be maintained. Resources should be used as effectively as possible, and the district should avoid programs and services that it cannot afford. The budget should reflect a strong commitment to maintain the school system's fiscal soundness. Third, school leaders must develop short- and long-range goals and priorities before developing the budget.

Each year, many important decisions are made that impact the budget. Whether to hire or replace staff, what fringe benefits to provide, salary adjustments for employees, new instructional programs, maintenance of facilities, and construction of new schools are just a few of the critical decisions that must be reached in the budget development process.

A good budgeting process provides for input from staff and community in a decentralized mode, while also ensuring that all legal requirements are met. In the past many districts relied upon an authoritarian mode of budgeting, making all decisions at the superintendent and governing board level. Today, budgets typically begin in a decentralized process, with input from every school and department. This approach has its own failings, however, since limited resources mean that many requests cannot be honored.

THE STATE BUDGET CALENDAR

The adoption of the state budget starts with the governor's presentation of the budget. This presentation is made in early January of each year. Next, the legislature is required to approve and submit a budget to the governor by June 15 of each year. This constitutional deadline has been met only three times since 1976, twice in the 80s and once in the 90s. The 1992-93 state budget set a record by being 64 days late; in that year the state was forced to pay some of its bills with IOUs. Lawmakers assess themselves no penalty for their tardiness, but state agencies begin to feel the effects of a budget stalemate after July 1. The adoption calendar for the state budget is contained in Table 2.

TABLE 2

Typical State Budget Adoption Calendar

January . . . . Governor proposes budget for following years

Late February . . . . Legislative Analyst releases budget analysis

March/April . . . . Legislative Sub-Committee hearings on the budget

Mid-May . . . . Governor proposes revisions of budget

Late May . . . . Full Committees approve budget; each House adopts budget

Early June . . . . Conference Committee approves budget; each House adopts budget

June 15 . . . . Constitutional deadline for Legislature to adopt budget

June 30 . . . . Constitutional deadline for Governor to sign budget

THE DISTRICT BUDGET CALENDAR

The first step in developing the budget calendar is to let everyone know the sequence of events and deadlines for decision-making. Timetables vary from district to district, but the basic steps are the same, no matter what time of year the cycle is started. The budget calendar, which should be approved by the governing board no later than October or November of each year, is a key document that guides actions of the district throughout the year. The budget calendar should detail dates when budget additions and reductions are reviewed, when worksheets are due in the business office, and when important policy decisions are made. Another feature of the budget calendar is identification of the administrator responsible for each task. Lacking such assignments, tasks to be accomplished by a certain date may be overlooked because no person is accountable for their completion.

The budget calendar should include a deadline for enrollment projections. Accuracy in this projection is fundamental to the accuracy of budget figures. The business officer may project enrollments centrally or may choose to have each principal responsible for estimating school enrollment for the following year. In either case, figures should be reviewed carefully.

It should be recognized that much debate over finances will ensue, even though a district has a budget calendar. With the recent emphasis on restructuring and site-based management, leading to numerous committees and meetings at school sites, many opinions will be expressed and many requests submitted. Given diminishing resources, it sometimes seems that groups and committees are engaged in a futile battle over dwindling assets. Thus, the budget calendar is not a panacea that solves financial problems, but a road map to meet legal requirements and to yield a cohesive plan for managing the district's financial resources. A typical district budget calendar, with timelines for adoption, is contained in Table 3.

BASIC LEGAL REQUIREMENTS GOVERNING BUDGET DEVELOPMENT

A significant budget law, AB 1200, was approved by the legislature and signed by the governor in 1991. This law was passed because several California districts found it necessary to obtain state loans to remain solvent. AB 1200 became effective January 1, 1992. It greatly increases the authority of each county superintendent of schools and of the state's Superintendent of Public Instruction. Each of these levels of government is authorized to review and monitor local school district budgets. AB 1200 particularly places

Table 3

Typical District Budget Adoption Calendar

On or before

July 1	Board holds public hearing, adopts budget, and files it with the county superintendent
August 15	If county superintendent approves budget, process ends
August 15	If county superintendent disapproves, budget is returned to district with comments
September 8	Dual adoption district holds public hearing, adopts revised budget, and resubmits it with responses to county superintendent
October 8	County superintendent approves or disapproves revised budget. If budget is disapproved, local board appoints a three-member budget review committee; the state superintendent is notified of this action
October 31	Budget review committee completes review of budget
October 31	District board may select single or dual adoption calendar for next year
October 31	Interim financial report is required by school district
November	If budget review committee disapproves budget, board has five days to submit response to state superintendent
November 30	If state superintendent disapproves budget, county superintendent develops budget for local school district
January 31	Second interim financial report is required by school district
February	School district develops budget guidelines for next fiscal year
March 15	District serves notice of intent to reduce site-level certificated management personnel (if needed)
March 15	District serves notice of intent to reduce teachers and central office certificated management personnel (if needed)
March 15	Budget worksheets are distributed to program administrators
April 1	District serves notice of intent to reduce classified staff (if needed)
May 1	Employees receive final notice of layoff (if needed)
May 1	Board adopts order to lay off employees
June	Staff presents budget for review by local school board

greater responsibility on the county superintendent for monitoring, and where necessary, intervening in school district fiscal matters. The law establishes a system of checks and balances to provide the board of education and the administration with early awareness of potential financial problems. It is also designed to facilitate assistance from the county level to local districts. Specifically, AB 1200

- changed the previous budget adoption process and timelines

- expanded the definition of solvency by addressing a district's ability to meet multi-year, and not just current year, commitments

- identified new local requirements to be met before ratification of collective bargaining agreements

- provided a new process to be followed if budgets are disapproved by the county superintendent of schools

- established stern consequences for failure to meet the above provisions.

School districts must end the year with a balanced budget. To ensure this condition, they are required to set aside a specified percent of the budget for economic uncertainties. The percentage depends upon district average daily attendance:

ADA	Required Set-Aside
300 or less	5%
300 to 1,000	4%
1,001 to 30,000	3%
30,001 to 400,000	2%
400,001 or more (Los Angeles)	1%

A district that is unable to meet the annual financial obligation may have no other recourse than to petition the state for an emergency loan. About 35 districts in California have received such loans, including Berkeley, Oakland, Richmond, West Contra Costa, West Covina, Coachella, and Compton. Montebello had to employ fiscal consultants to avoid bankruptcy. Several other districts, including Los Angeles, severely reduced expenditures to maintain a balanced budget and avoid a state loan or bankruptcy. As of 1999-2000, only three districts—West Contra Costa, Coachella, and Compton—still had outstanding loans, and no district required an emergency loan in 1999-2000 (Connell, 2000).

BUDGET PROCESS

AB 1200 eliminated the requirement that each school district submit a tentative budget. Instead, each district is required to adopt a budget by July 1. This legislation provides for a single or a dual budget adoption schedule. Districts that elect the single budget schedule must conduct a public hearing by July 1. Once the budget has been adopted, the district may revise the budget within 45 days after the governor signs the state budget. The July 1 date completes the process for single adoption districts. Supporters of this approach point out that the labor-intensive, often time-consuming, budget adoption process is cut in half. Single adoption is still flexible in that districts may make changes through budget revisions and the interim report process as additional information about revenues becomes available.

The dual adoption approach is similar to the process most districts have used for years. A first budget is adopted, without the requirement of a mandatory public hearing, by July 1. A second and final budget, which requires a public hearing, is adopted by September 1. Districts choosing the dual approach have two chances to put together a viable budget, once in July and again in August. This extra month gives districts opportunity to finalize ending balances and to obtain additional information about the state budget and district revenues. State statute requires public hearings on both single and dual adopted budgets, but the hearing is timed differently in each case. Both types of budget are reviewed by the county superintendent of schools, who has authority and responsibility to suggest changes in the budget.

FINANCIAL MANAGEMENT ADVISORY COMMITTEE (FMAC)

During the early 1980s the state was required to make short-term loans to avoid insolvency in several districts. Alameda County Office of Education, the Emeryville Unified School District, and the Berkeley Unified District borrowed money from the state during this time. As a result, the state legislature and controller directed the California Department of Education to establish an improved accounting system for California districts. In response to this directive, the Department of Education established a Financial Management Advisory Committee (FMAC) in 1983.

Prior to the work of this committee, forms used by school districts to account for budget revenue and expenditure varied widely. FMAC was charged with the task of developing uniform financial reporting forms and accounting systems for use by all California districts. The FMAC system required new reports to provide an early warning system of impending financial difficulty. Since 1988-89 all California districts and county offices of education have used this system.

Just five years later, in 1993, Senate Bill 94 was approved by the legislature and signed by the governor. The bill required the California Department of Education to prepare a report to the legislature by September 1, 1994, regarding development and statewide implementation of a new K-12 accounting and reporting structure. This legislation was developed in response to state and federal pressure for a model with greater fiscal accountability, public disclosure, and availability of site- and program-level financial data for comparison within and among districts and states. The uniform account structure called for by FMAC was developed in 1994-95. In 1996 the California Department of Education issued a request for proposals from school accounting providers to implement the new structure. The California Educational Computer Consortium along with three other consortia submitted a proposal that was accepted by the state. Beginning in the 1998-99 school year, all California districts were using the new account structure.

INTERIM FINANCIAL REPORTS

Interim financial reports have been required for the past several years. The state requires that boards certify in October and again in January that their finances are in good shape. However, AB 1200 gives substantial new authority to the county superintendent of schools when reviewing these reports. Three classes of certification were established:

- **Positive Certification**—This certification means that the district has sufficient resources to meet its financial obligations for the current or two subsequent years.

- **Qualified Certification**—This certification means that the district may or may not have sufficient resources to meet its financial obligations for the current or subsequent fiscal year.

- **Negative Certification**—This certification means that the district does not have the resources to meet its financial obligations for the remainder of the fiscal year or the subsequent fiscal year.

These reports are submitted to the county superintendent, with negative reports sent to the California Department of Education. When a district certifies a negative financial report, the county superintendent has the authority to develop and adopt a budget for the district. The county superintendent also may rescind any financial action that is inconsistent with that budget. Districts with a qualified or negative certification may not issue certificates of participation, tax anticipation notes, revenue bonds, or any other debt instrument not requiring voter approval.

CHARACTERISTICS OF INEFFECTIVE BUDGETING

Stan Oswalt, a former California superintendent and a state-appointed fiscal advisor, developed a description of five characteristics of ineffective budgeting:

- **Ineffective estimations of ending balances**—Accounts receivable are overestimated, and accounts payable are underestimated.

- **Ineffective budget development**—Federal, state, and local income are overestimated, and expenditures are underestimated. Also, adequate reserves for economic uncertainties are not maintained.

- **Ineffective budget monitoring and reporting**—The budget is not adjusted as revenues are reduced. Adequate information for management decisions is not made available, and planned expenditures are not encumbered. Also, encroachment of restricted programs on the General Fund is not reduced.

- **Ineffective attendance accounting**—Average daily attendance is not projected accurately, and adjustments are not made for inaccurate reporting.

- **Ineffective personnel practices**—The staff of the business or personnel office fail to adequately maintain personnel records. Multi-year personnel contracts exist, and precise cost of positions is not maintained.

In addition to the characteristics of ineffective budgeting, Oswalt also identified several danger signals that may result in financial insolvency:

- **Cash flow problems**—Districts headed for financial problems often have need to borrow from other sources before they turn to the state. When the borrowing is based on unrealistic revenue or expenditure projections, the district runs out of cash.

- **Small beginning and ending balances**—Without an adequate beginning and ending balance, the district greatly reduces its ability to cope with unforeseen circumstances.

- **Unrealistic collective bargaining contracts**—This factor led to near insolvency in Los Unified School District. As a result of a strike, certificated employees were granted a 24% raise over a three-year period. When the COLA from the state was significantly less than the pay increase, the district found itself in a very difficult financial situation. Multi-year contracts without ties to revenues or expenditures and without a re-opener pose great financial danger to a district.

- **Turnover in administration**—Turnover in key positions such as superintendent, chief business official, or director of accounting affects consistency of management in a district. Oswalt states that a turnover rate of more than three chief business officials and/or superintendents in five years may indicate a financial problem.

- **Lack of experience in key personnel**—The background and experience of the superintendent and chief business official and other key people in the business office can have a significant effect on the successful financial operation of the district.

- **Lax internal controls**—If clear and concise controls are not in place, unwise decisions may be made about expenditures.

- **Inadequate financial review**—Financial reports must be frequent and reliable if the school board and superintendent are to make quality decisions. Financial reports should be presented in open session of the board of education and should be in writing, never just verbal.

- **Internal political struggles**—Political struggles make it difficult for strong, positive, and continuing leadership to exist. Board members assuming the role of the superintendent or other key administrative personnel may signal serious problems.

- **Enrollment decline**—It is often difficult for a district to adjust to declining enrollment. School board members and the superintendent may be reluctant to make the hard decisions to reduce staff and programs. Closure of schools, which may be needed in the face of declining enrollment, may also be a political decision that puts the district at financial risk (Oswalt, 1992).

FISCAL ADVISORS

Under AB 1200 the county superintendent may assign fiscal advisors to a district that has been determined unable to meet its financial obligations. The communication to the district from the county office begins with a meeting between a county staff member and the district superintendent and business staff. After this discussion, the committee meets with the governing board. Districts that are unable to avoid fiscal insolvency may receive an emergency state apportionment, but only as a last resort. When this action is taken, the state superintendent appoints a trustee to supervise the district. The trustee reports directly to the state superintendent until the loan is repaid.

REVENUE ESTIMATION FOR THE NEXT YEAR

A budget calendar provides a blueprint for timing certain reports and projections. Usually by December or January of each school year, the business office has received sufficient fiscal information about the subsequent year's income to begin the process of revenue estimation. These are the best months in which to begin the tough job of estimating the following year's income.

The CBO must rely on two major sources of information that are available in December. One source is the monthly expenditure reports that have been generated for the first six months of the fiscal year. The second source of information is average daily attendance (ADA) reports or actual student attendance; with these, the business department determines trends from which to project the all-important enrollment for the subsequent year. More specific calculations related to income are described in the following sections.

ENROLLMENT PROJECTIONS. Enrollment projections are significant not only because they indicate income, but also because they determine classroom usage and the number of teaching positions needed. All districts should prepare at least five- to ten-year projections for enrollment, income, and expenditures. Even if the income formula changes, having a plan that can be adjusted is much better than having no plan at all. Long-range projections accustom the staff to long-range planning. This activity sets up a mode of thinking ahead that is good practice for all staff members, helping them break out of the status quo to anticipate and prepare for foreseeable changes.

ADA PROJECTIONS. Most of a district's revenue has been based not on enrollment, but on ADA, average daily attendance. This figure is calculated as the number of days students in the district are actually in class plus the number of excused absences, divided by the number of school days:

$$\frac{\text{DAYS ATTENDING CLASS + EXCUSED ABSENCES}}{\text{TOTAL SCHOOL DAYS}} = ADA$$

If, for example, 1,000 students were in class or excused (ill) every school day in a 184-day school year, that would yield 184,000 for the numerator of the equation. Dividing that figure by 184 school days = 1000 ADA. If some of the students were not excused because they cut class or their absence was not verified as illness, etc., one might have only 180,200 in the numerator, yielding 979.3 ADA.

Most districts use percentages from 96% to 98% of projected enrollment to estimate ADA because there are always unicast absences. Thus, once enrollment has been estimated, the ADA can be determined.

ACTUAL-ATTENDANCE CALCULATION BEGINNING 1998-99. Prior to the 1998-1999 school year, all school districts and county offices received state dollars for every day that a student actually attended classes. As explained in the preceding section, districts also received funds for excused absences, usually illness. Since fall of 1998, districts only receive funding for days students are actually in class. This new procedure is known as "actual attendance accounting." The objective of making the change was to give districts an incentive to maximize student attendance and to decrease absences for any cause.

To make the transition from ADA to actual attendance accounting, the daily rate for student attendance was increased on a district-by-district basis by an amount equal to each district's excused absence rate for the 1996-1997 school year. For example, a district that had a 5% excused absence rate in 1996-1997 could no longer receive funding for the 5% excused absences, but received an additional 5% in funding for each student who actually attended school.

This formula may be compared with that in the preceding section.

$$\frac{\text{DAYS ATTENDING CLASS}}{\text{TOTAL SCHOOL DAYS}} = ActualAttendance$$

COST OF LIVING ADJUSTMENT (COLA). Proposition 98 provides an overall minimum allocation to education of 40% of state revenues, but the COLA is the increased amount per ADA that is apportioned to individual districts. Commonly, amounts from 3% to 5% are identified as COLA in the governor's budget. The COLA is used in a formula with ADA to determine each district's total revenue limit amount, which is the largest income block assigned to each district.

CATEGORICAL REVENUE. Categorical funds are those earmarked for specific purposes such as the child nutrition program, gifted and talented education, and driver training. Typically, these programs receive an increase known as the statutory COLA, applied as a flat percentage of the preceding year's entitlement.

For several years 30 categorical funds have been combined into a single budget "Mega-Item," originally proposed to prevent the governor from vetoing dollar amounts for individual programs as well as to allow flexibility in transferring dollars among programs. Districts may spend the block of money for any or all of the programs making up the Mega-Item. For example, a district could take money from home-to-school transportation, reallocating it to instructional materials or educational technology. However, although the Mega-Item programs are combined for budget purposes, each of the programs has guidelines defining its purpose and describing how the money may be spent. Students eligible for any of these programs must be served as required by law.

This concept has been continued each year. In 2000-01 districts were allowed to transfer up to 20% away from any program in the categorical Mega-Item and up to 25% into any program in the Mega-Item. However, several programs, including special education, adult education, child development, regional occupational programs, and K-8 and 9-12 funds for instructional materials, were excluded. The Mega-Item continues to be controversial because it challenges the philosophy under which most categorical programs were instituted in the first place—that is, to meet special and unique needs of students and teachers that were not being addressed with general purpose monies.

SPECIAL EDUCATION INCOME. Funding for special education comes from various sources, including federal, state, and local aid. Special education programs that receive funds include Designated Instructional Services (pullout model), Resource Specialist (pullout model), Special Day Classes (placement in special day class with other services), placement in nonpublic facilities, and state special education schools.

LOTTERY INCOME. The California State Lottery Act (Proposition 37) was approved by the voters in 1984 and implemented by the state legislature in 1985. The Lottery Act states that the purpose of the California lottery is to generate funding to supplement the public education budget to the extent of at least 34% of sales. The funds are distributed to several sectors of public education, including K-12 school districts, community colleges, and county offices of education.

Typically, public education has received 36% to 39% of proceeds, the larger figures as a result of savings in administration and unclaimed prizes. Of lottery proceeds, 50% is returned to players as prizes, and 16% may be used to administer the lottery. This allocation translates to roughly 2% to 3% of a school district's General Fund budget.

The upside of this income is that it may be spent for any purpose except construction or purchase of buildings. A minor change was made in permissible expenditures in March of 2000. California voters approved Proposition 20, which requires that 1/2 the annual increase in state lottery funds be spent on instructional materials.

The downside is its unreliability. Since lottery income is dependent upon the interest of citizens and varies from game to game, revenue from this source is very difficult to predict accurately. Lottery income reached a high of $178 per pupil in 1988-89, but dropped sharply to $77 for 1991-92. It was projected at $120 for 2000-2001. Figure 5 contains information on distribution of lottery funds from 1985-86 through 1999-2000 (California Lottery Commission, 2000).

Even though lottery estimates are placed into a district's final budget document, quarterly reports are necessary to update income and expenditures and keep the budget on target. It may be necessary to make further adjustments as the year progresses.

ESTIMATION OF THE FOLLOWING YEAR'S EXPENSES

Once revenue has been estimated, all expenses for the coming year must also be estimated. Costs may be divided into those that can be controlled and those that cannot. Costs also may be divided into personnel and non-personnel items. The collective bargaining agreement should be reviewed carefully for costs that may be "hidden," but were nonetheless negotiated and must be included in the budget. Examples of expenses that must be estimated and placed in the budget are described below.

Figure 5

California State Lottery

Total K-12 Lottery Allocation per ADA

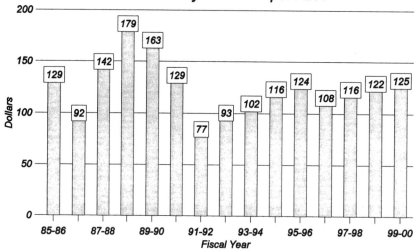

CERTIFICATED SALARIES. Teacher salaries are calculated according to the negotiated percentage increase. On certificated salary schedules in most California districts, the cost of step and column increases also must be estimated. This cost may range from 2% to 4% of the amount budgeted for certificated salaries. Teacher substitutes are also provided for in this category.

CLASSIFIED SALARIES. Instructional aides are assigned to individual programs. Also budgeted under classified salaries are clerical staff and personnel for transportation and maintenance. Added to these costs are substitute personnel for these workers. Most classified salary schedules include step or anniversary increases that must also be factored into the calculations.

EMPLOYEE BENEFITS. Funds are budgeted here for the State Teachers' Retirement System, the Public Employees' Retirement System, workers' compensation, and health and welfare benefits. A percentage is used to estimate most of these expenses. The amount for health and welfare is typically a negotiated figure in the collective bargaining agreement.

If long-term retirement benefits have been negotiated, they should be included in these accounts.

BOOKS AND SUPPLIES. All instructional materials, textbooks, and transportation supplies are budgeted here. Usually, it is best to develop allocation formulas for different situations so conflict does not become the cornerstone of these accounts. For example, instructional materials may be budgeted at a different amount per student depending upon whether the pupil is in elementary, junior high, or high school. Textbook allotments from the state are included in this category; a major item in this account is adoption of new textbooks, which follows an eight-year cycle.

UTILITIES, CONTRACTS, AND INSURANCE COSTS. Utilities are usually estimated by applying an inflation percentage to each. Contracts also should be listed in this budget area. Property and liability premiums are included in this account, along with travel and conference expenses and dues and memberships.

CAPITAL OUTLAY. Both new and replacement equipment should appear in the capital outlay budget.

TUITION. Any type of outgoing tuition should be included in this account. A reserve of at least 3% to 5% should be budgeted in this section.

The most important point about calculating income and expenditures is that it is completed early enough to accommodate adjustments. If the first calculation is made in December or January, then debate can ensue, allowing for timely submission of the tentative and final budgets.

COMMUNITY AND INDIVIDUAL SCHOOL PARTICIPATION

Because of the current emphasis upon the concept of restructuring, much effort is given to beginning budget discussions at school sites. Actually, districts that are successful in implementing restructuring employ both decentralized and centralized budgeting procedures.

SCHOOL SITE DECENTRALIZATION. Committees are typically formed at the school site to discuss all budget policies related to that site. These discussions may address topics ranging from staffing to use of the copy machine. Most often, the school principal forms these committees and participates in committee discussions and recommendations. He or she should be influential in reviewing community and staff recommendations and deciding which may be useful and which not.

Inevitably, some suggestions will conflict with policies imposed by central office budgeting decisions. For example, teachers might like a class ratio of 20 students to one teacher, or perhaps discretionary use of all lottery funds. However, because of finite resources, restructuring committees must realize at the start that certain desires at the school site cannot be fulfilled. Nevertheless, the discussions and debate are, in and of themselves, a valuable tool for building teamsmanship. In addition, one of the main tenets of site-based management is the formation of "responsible parties." Planning for change within inevitable constraints, even though some actions cannot be accomplished at once, helps that responsibility to mature.

CENTRALIZED BUDGETING MODE. Even in a centralized budgeting mode, budget sheets and computer printouts are typically distributed to each school principal and collected by the business staff to be included in the budget. Site income may be centrally determined, but distribution across expenditure categories is somewhat flexible. In any case, the governing board has the final decision in structuring the school district budget, even though the board may solicit input from the superintendent and staff.

SUMMARY

The school district budget serves as a blueprint or master plan for the district. It should be a document that clearly establishes priorities for the district. A successful budget requires skill and expertise on the part of the business staff who project revenues and expenditures. Outstanding leadership and communication skills also are required by the board, superintendent, and principals as they involve staff, parents, and the community in developing this document.

AB 1200 is a mandate to school districts that unwise or imprudent financial decisions leading toward insolvency will not be tolerated. The law clearly and forcefully takes authority away from local boards who endanger the solvency of public schools.

Budgeting is a political, as well as rational, issue. The district budget is a spending *plan*. It establishes the priorities and objectives of a district and a community. A cursory examination of a district's budget reveals the priorities of the district. What, for example, is the level of support for school athletics—or for music? What attention is paid to landscaping and maintenance of facilities? What is the level of support for the college preparatory curriculum and the vocational education program? Questions like these reflect a community's commitment to programs and priorities.

In most districts the process of budget development calls for participation by many groups in the district. The governing board typically listens to all groups and makes decisions by balancing their beliefs against the fiscal constraints imposed upon them.

KEY TERMS

AB 1200	Interim financial reports
District budget calendar	Legislative Analyst
Enrollment projections	Spending plan
FMAC	State budget calendar

DISCUSSION/ESSAY QUESTIONS

1. The district budget is a plan for accomplishing the educational objectives of the district. Discuss three necessary budget priorities for accomplishing this objective.

2. Although the state legislature is required to submit a budget to the governor by June 15, this requirement is rarely met. Discuss major reasons for failure of the legislature to meet this deadline and suggest remedies to ensure compliance.

3. The district budget calendar is a management plan to ensure development of an optimum budget. Discuss the major components that should be included in a successful budget calendar.

4. All California districts are required to submit two interim financial reports each year to the County Superintendent of Schools. The County Superintendent has authority to establish one of three certifications for each interim report. Discuss the three certifications and the significance of each.

5. There are several clues that a district may be practicing ineffective budgeting procedures. Discuss three major problems that characterize ineffective district budgeting.

6. California has had a state lottery since 1985. Discuss the advantages and disadvantages of utilizing lottery income to support schools.

7. Decentralization of the budget to school sites is becoming a trend in California. What are the major advantages and disadvantages of this process?

CHAPTER 6

PROGRAM BUDGETING
AND EXPENDITURES ACCOUNTING

INTRODUCTION

Districts concerned with the costs of operating diverse programs utilize program budgeting. This system allocates income and expenditures to specific cost centers. Districts use a system of account codes to identify specific costs by program or department. Account codes have recently been redefined by the California Department of Education. As described later in this chapter, they now incorporate seven elements: fund/group, resource, project year, goal, function, object, and school. Specific accounting details for program budgeting, including revenue and expenditures codes, are found in the latest edition of the *California School Accounting Manual*. The manual may be ordered in hard copy from the California Department of Education or obtained online at http://www.cde.ca.gov/fiscal/sacs/csam2000/

Typically, a district maintains a chart of accounts to interpret the financial reports of the district. For example, to track costs of the gifted and talented program in a district over a three-year period, program budgeting would enable one to collect all program income and expenditure figures for this span of time. Typically, school districts tie goals and objectives to program budgets, being careful to analyze the cost of achieving agreed-upon objectives.

Program budgeting is designed to provide school district decision-makers, the public, and the legislature with detailed information about the services and benefits purchased by a district. Program budgeting assumes that each program will be assessed periodically to determine its usefulness and effectiveness. To this end, program expenditures are evaluated in conjunction with the district's goals and objectives. This information assists the superintendent and governing board to decide whether to eliminate, reduce, or increase the funding of a particular program.

There are four types of program budgeting: incremental or historical, zero-based, planned program budget system, and site-based. Incremental or historical budgeting has the longest track record of building budgets in the public and private sector. Budget reformers of the 1960s, 1970s, and 1980s attempted to institute new types of program budgeting into public school systems, though with but partial success.

INCREMENTAL OR HISTORICAL BUDGETING

Budgeting in most school districts is incremental, or historical. The starting point in incremental budgeting is the prior year budget. The previous year's allocation for each budget item is increased or decreased by a particular percentage. Decisions are made for each existing line item, either to add or subtract dollars, to carry the item forward unchanged, or to delete it entirely. The vast bulk of expenditures continue year after year, budget cycle after budget cycle. Under this system, allocations change very little from year to year.

The rationale for incremental budgeting is that the major portion of a district's budget is allocated to salaries and benefits. District decision-makers feel they have little latitude for significant changes in other expenditures. An advantage of the incremental approach is its relative simplicity. Certain "fixed" costs—such as utilities, insurance, and supplies—are easily adjusted. Salaries and benefits can be projected and calculated. This system also creates less anxiety on the part of employees, who may fear that more detailed budget scrutiny could result in discontinuance of a particular program. The major disadvantage to incremental budgeting is that it may not respond to changing district needs. As a consequence, existing programs may continue beyond their usefulness and, unless new funds or resources become available, institution of new programs is likely to be difficult.

PLANNING-PROGRAMMING-BUDGETING SYSTEM (PPBS)

In the 1960s, Robert McNamara, then Secretary of Defense, introduced a systems analysis approach at the Defense Department. His hope was this system would provide decision-makers with more reliable information in the budgeting process. This *planning-programming-budgeting system* became known as PPBS. McNamara, who had been an executive at Ford Motor Company, believed that PPBS would provide more precise evaluation of the outcome of programs. The success of the process prompted other government departments to institute similar planning techniques.

PPBS is a centralized budgeting system. With this approach, goals are established at the district level, with budget development proceeding downward to departments and school sites. The primary objective of PPBS is to provide decision-makers with more complete, accurate, and objective information for planning educational programs and for choosing among alternatives in spending funds to achieve educational objectives. Program budgeting assumes that each program, or at least a significant portion of programs, will be assessed periodically to determine their usefulness and effectiveness. Programs that are judged as not meeting agreed-upon objectives would then be improved or eliminated.

An early criticism of PPBS was a felt lack of evaluation in the system. Consequently, evaluation was added, making the system PPBES. The Association of School Business Officials attempted to make the system more compatible with school district budgeting practices and renamed it ERMD (Educational Resource Management Division).

The major advantage of PPBS lies in providing a way to measure limited resources against the objectives of the district and subsequently to retain and reject programs that are or are not in concert with objectives. In addition, PPBS fosters a long-term view by extending the planning period and duration of program budgeting to five or more years. A major disadvantage of this system is the enormous amount of data that must be collected and the time-consuming task of analyzing the data. A second disadvantage in the system is that it is top-down, driven by major objectives established at the district board level.

ZERO-BASED BUDGETING (ZBB)

Arthur Burns, former chairman of the Federal Reserve Board, is generally credited with the first public use of the term zero-based budgeting (ZBB); that was in 1969. However, the concept of ZBB was actually initiated by Peter A. Phyrr, a manager at Texas Instruments. Rather than continue the allocation of funds for each program year after year, Texas Instruments decided to begin each year from ground zero. The objective was to review all programs, and thus to improve allocations for the subsequent year. This type of budgeting received additional attention in 1979, when President Carter issued an executive order directing each federal agency to submit budget requests following the ZBB format.

In contrast to PPBS, zero-based budgeting builds from the bottom-up. The basic concept of ZBB is that all administrators reassess their programs annually. The one cardinal principle for ZBB is that nothing is sacred. Every program, if it is to receive funding, must be justified during each budget development cycle. Budget requests are ranked and justified by the principal or supervisor and forwarded to the next level. The administrator is asked to provide justification for the financial resources requested to meet program goals. Final decisions are made by the school board and superintendent. The objective of ZBB is to force a rigorous evaluation of all programs. Once each program has been subjected to the evaluation procedure, it may be continued, discontinued, or modified—with appropriate allocation of resources.

There are several advantages of this type budgeting, including involvement of teachers and staff members, the required annual evaluation of all programs, and the development of priorities with alternatives. As with PPBS, critics of ZBB point to the great amount of paperwork involved in the process and the need for more administrative time in the preparation of the budget. Thus, a disadvantage is the feeling that the system is too complicated and impractical for school districts. Prior commitments created by collective bargaining contracts, teacher tenure, and committed funds for school construction also make a true form of zero-based budgeting very difficult for districts.

SITE-BASED BUDGETING (SBB)

School principals and teachers have always had some discretion over particular elements of the school budget. Such items have included school supplies, textbooks, and—to a limited extent—expenditures for capital equipment. The recent trend, however, is to allow greater discretion in budget development, including such categories as staffing and capital improvements, to decision-makers at the school site. For example, schools in such a district may have latitude to purchase the services of two teacher aides in place of one certificated teacher, or to employ a music specialist rather than a reading teacher.

Site-based budgeting (SBB) is a practice wherein teachers, staff, community members, and administrators develop the budget at the school site. SBB has as its primary objective to match student needs to available resources. It places decision-making at the level nearest students, in the hands of teachers and staff who will implement the decisions. In California, charter schools and restructuring are two programs designed to place greater authority at the site level, in the hands of the principal, staff, and community members. School-level decision-makers, usually the principal assisted by a School Advisory Council of teachers and parents, decide on allocation of resources.

SBB appears to have several advantages. It can provide site participants greater latitude in matching local needs and objectives with available and resources. In addition, it may improve morale and motivation of staff and community members at the local school. By its very nature, decentralized budgeting nature forces wider participation in program planning. Acknowledging the unique culture of each particular school and staff, SBB brings together the principal, teachers, staff, community members, and—in secondary schools, at least—students to develop an improved educational program for their school. It tends to allow greater innovation in programs than does a centralized budgeting process.

Critics of SBB charge that it may compartmentalize education in the community. Each school may become independent of the district and settle for a narrow focus of goals and objectives. Rivalry and competition could take the place of cooperation among schools within the district. In addition, pressure groups may be able to exert greater control over the school. If these pitfalls are to be avoided, so that site budgeting achieves its objectives, decision-makers in the district and at the school site must establish clear policies and effective communication links.

HISTORY OF THE *CALIFORNIA SCHOOL ACCOUNTING MANUAL*

All California school districts are required to monitor and account accurately for all revenues and expenditures. The California Department of Education has responsibility for developing proper forms and procedures for school district accounting.

The first manual for school accounting was developed in 1939 based on information provided by the U.S. Office of Education. This early document contained information on proper accounting procedures for the classification of expenditures as well as definitions of accounting terms. Over the intervening several decades the manual has been revised many times to meet the needs of school districts, the state department, state legislature, governor, school boards, and interested citizens. Added sections have expanded definitions of expenditures, clarified the difference between "supplies" and "equipment," and described accounting procedures to purchase school sites and construct school buildings.

Current procedures are contained in the *California School Accounting Manual*, which the California Department of Education developed with the assistance and cooperation of the California Association of School Business Officials (CASBO). This chapter draws information from the 2000 edition of the manual. As accounting procedures change and new laws are passed, the manual is revised; revisions are posted on the Website of the California Department of Education (http://www.cde.ca.gov). Ordering information and the URL for the complete manual were given at the beginning of this chapter.

CALIFORNIA'S ACCOUNT CODE STRUCTURE

The objectives of a standardized school accounting structure are contained in the *California School Accounting Manual*. They are briefly summarized as follows:

- to establish a uniform, comprehensive chart of accounts to improve financial data collection, reporting, transmission, accuracy, and comparability

- to reduce the workload of school employees in preparing financial reports

- to meet federal compliance requirements and to increase opportunities for California districts to receive federal funding

- to ensure that school districts conform to generally accepted accounting principles (GAAP)

- to inform stakeholders of the sources of funds and how they are used.

To accomplish these objectives, the account code structure contains six fields that must be included in the accounting structure of all districts. These fields are:

Fund/Account Group   Resource   Project Year
Goal   Function (Activity)   Object

A seventh field, "school," was optional for districts in the 2000-2001 school year. California districts are permitted to add additional fields in their chart of accounts, but must include the required six. The fields are briefly described:

- **Fund**—Identifies specific activities or defines objectives of the district. Examples include the general fund, adult education fund, and transportation fund. Additional discussion of funds is contained in Chapter 8.

- **Account Group**—A group of accounts for fixed assets or for the general long-term debt of the district. Fixed assets are of a permanent character, having something of value, e.g., land, buildings, machinery, furniture, and equipment. Long-term debt may include outstanding bonds, long-term notes, and capital leases. Long-term debts are usually incurred when a district borrows funds to purchase land or equipment or for construction.

- **Resource**—Established for revenues that have special accounting or reporting requirements or that have legal requirements as to how the funds may be used. Examples include federal programs, lottery funds, and the State Building Fund.

- **Project Year**—Used for projects that span more than one fiscal year. Typically, this category includes federal grants. An example from the accounting manual includes a bilingual grant from October 1 (the start of the federal fiscal year) 1997 through September 30, 1998, and a second grant from October 1, 1998 through September 30, 1999. Grant activities for state fiscal year 1998-1999 would include three months of expenditures for the first grant and nine months of expenditures for the second grant.

- **Goal**—Tracks income and expenditures by the district's instructional goals. Examples include regular classes, classes for gifted students, driver training, and vocational education.

- **Function**—Tracks income and expenditures for services performed to accomplish one or more objectives in the goal field. An example contained in the accounting manual relates to school transportation. To educate students, a district must transport them to school, feed them, and provide health services. Each of these activities is a function.

- **Object**—Tracks expenditures by the service or commodity. Examples include salaries, employee benefits, books and supplies, services, capital outlay, and a section entitled "other outgo."

- **School**—Enables the district to track expenditures at a specific physical structure or school. Examples might include Washington Elementary School and the District Office.

An example of using the account codes is presented in the state accounting manual.

Fund/Group	Resource	Project Year	Goal	Function	Object	School
01	7155	0	1110	1000	4100	123

In this example,

Fund 01	is the General Fund
Resource 7155	is Instructional Materials, grades K-8
Project Year	is not required in this example
Goal 1110	is Regular Education, K-12
Function 1000	is Instruction
Object 4100	is Approved Textbooks and Core Curricula Materials
School 123	is the ABC Elementary School.

SCHOOL DISTRICT EXPENDITURES

The greatest expenditure of California tax dollars goes to support education. In 2001-2002 expenditures for kindergarten through twelfth-grade education were budgeted at 41% of the state budget, while higher education took an additional 13%. After education, the next highest budget area was health and social services at 28% (Hill, 2001).

Expenditures decrease net spendable resources. Expenditures include operating expenses; payments toward retirement of long-term debt; and capital outlay for long-term assets such as land, buildings, and equipment. The Education Code limits school district expenditures to the amounts appropriated for the several major expenditure classes by the board of education through the adoption, approval, and revision of the school district budget. The budget and all documents dealing with appropriations must be prepared in accordance with the same classifications to account for expenditures. To facilitate necessary comparisons, financial reports for local use, as well as those prepared for county, state, or federal agencies, follow the same classification plan.

OBJECTS OF EXPENDITURE

Objects of expenditure represent all the things, whether goods or services, that may be purchased. The object classification number identifies the type of item purchased or services obtained. All district operational expenses are included in the object codes. Examples include salaries, supplies, and equipment. In the budget document itself, objects of expenditure may be classified in various ways. They may be grouped under summary headings, or they may be presented in great detail. Grouping under summary headings reduces volume, but at the expense of clarity. Greater detail improves understanding, but is costly to produce. In practice, whatever the budget document may look like, the figures are backed up with highly detailed information on income and expenditures. Then, for reporting purposes, this detail is summarized under more general budget classifications.

Districts classify each expenditure by designating the appropriate goal, function, and object codes on requisitions. The principal or department supervisor is responsible for designating the object code when a requisition is completed. However, the district's chief accountant or business manager makes the final decision regarding the classification appropriate for each expenditure. This decision should be made at the time of commitment to the expenditure. The account or accounts to be charged should be selected whenever goods or services are ordered or when certificated or classified employees are employed or reassigned.

Notices of employment, copies of contracts, and other documents relating to expenditures, or to commitments that will become expenditures, should bear the relevant code designations for review and approval by the district governing board and the county superintendent of schools. This information should also be available for the district's auditor. This procedure ensures that questions concerning the classification of expenditures are settled promptly. A decision regarding object classifications may save time in the future if it serves for repeated disbursements, such as monthly salary payments. Such a procedure is vital if the encumbrance plan of accounting is used by the school district. Following are some of the more frequently used object codes.

<u>1000-1900 CERTIFICATED PERSONNEL SALARIES</u>. Certificated salaries are paid for positions that require a credential or permit issued by the Commission on Teacher Credentialing. All full-time, part-time, and prorated portions of salaries for personnel serving in these job classifications must be charged to the appropriate object code. Salaries paid to an employee on leave of absence are charged in the same manner and to the same account classification applicable while the employee was in active service for the district.

- **1100 Certificated Salaries**—The 1100 series of object codes is used to record the full-time, part-time, and prorated portions of salaries for all certificated personnel employed to teach the pupils of the district. The salaries for teachers of children in homes or hospitals, all special education resource specialists and teachers, substitute teachers, and instructional television teachers are included in this classification.

- **1200 Certificated Pupil Support Salaries**—This series of object codes is applied to salaries of librarians, social workers, pupil personnel specialists, psychologists and psychometrists, and counselors. Other salaries include those of physicians and other medical professionals.

- **1300 Certificated Supervisors' and Administrators' Salaries**—The salaries of full-time and part-time certificated personnel engaged in instructional supervision are included in this classification. Job titles include superintendent, associate and assistant superintendent, general supervisor, coordinator, director, and consultant, as well as supervisors of special subjects or grades and their certificated assistants. Duties of personnel who are paid from this classification involve activities intended to improve instruction. Examples include personal conferences with teachers on instructional problems, classroom visitations, group conferences with teachers, and demonstration teaching.

- **1900 Other Certificated Salaries**—The 1900 classification is assigned to all certificated personnel who do not fall within one of the categories previously specified. Examples of such personnel are special education or other program specialists, certificated civic center employees, resource teachers not performing duties as a classroom teacher, and certificated noon playground supervisors.

<u>2000-2999 CLASSIFIED PERSONNEL SALARIES</u>. Classified salaries cover positions that do not require a credential or permit issued by the Commission on Teacher

Credentialing. All full-time, part-time, and prorated portions of these salaries are charged to the object codes indicated.

- **2100 Instructional Aides' Salaries**—Salaries paid to instructional aides are charged to this classification. Instructional aides are those employees who perform their duties under the supervision of a classroom teacher or a special education resource specialist teacher.

- **2200 Classified Support Salaries**—This code is used to record the salaries of transportation, food service, maintenance and operations, and instructional media and library employees.

- **2300 Classified Supervisors' and Administrators' Salaries**—Job classifications in this category include supervisory personnel who are business managers, controllers, directors, chief accountants, supervisors, purchasing agents, assistant superintendents, and noncertificated superintendents. Governing board members and personnel commission members, if they receive district compensation, are also charged to this account.

- **2400 Clerical and Other Office Salaries**—All salaries of clerks, secretaries, accountants, bookkeepers, machine and computer operators, and personnel in similar positions are charged to this object code.

- **2900 Other Classified Salaries**—All classified salaries not identifiable with object classifications 2100 through 2400 are charged to this object code. Examples include noon supervision personnel, students, community aides, health aides, library aides, and building inspectors.

3000-3999 EMPLOYEE BENEFITS. The 3000 accounts are used for employers' contributions to retirement plans and health and welfare benefits. This classification is also designated for cash in lieu of benefits for employees, their dependents, retired employees, and board members.

4000-4999 BOOKS AND SUPPLIES. This classification is used for basic textbooks and instructional materials and supplies.

- **4100 Approved Textbooks and Core Curricular Materials**—This account is used for purchase of basic textbooks and supplementary textbooks. Related teacher manuals and teacher editions are also charged to this account. A basic textbook is defined as a volume intended for use by pupils as a principal source of study material for the completion of a subject or course. A supplementary textbook is a volume that covers part or all of a subject or course, but is not intended for use as a basic textbook. Rather, a supplementary textbook is intended to supply information in addition to, or in extension of, information presented in the regular, or basic, text. All approved consumable materials including kits, audiovisual materials, and workbooks are charged to this account.

- **4200 Books and Reference Materials**—This classification is used for books and other reference materials used by district personnel. Library books are also included in this category. However, expenditures for school library books for a new school library or for expansion are recorded under object classification 6300, Books and Media for New School Libraries or Major Expansion of School Libraries.

- **4300 Materials and Supplies**— Expenditures for all materials and supplies to be used by students, teachers, and other personnel in connection with the instructional program are charged to this classification. Tests, periodicals, magazines, workbooks, instructional media materials, audiovisual materials, and any other supplies used in the classroom or library are included in this category. Supplies for food service, custodial, gardening, maintenance, medical, and office supplies are also charged to this account. However, expenditures for rental of materials are recorded under object classification 5600, Rentals, Leases, and Repairs.

- **4700 Food**—This classification is used to record expenditures for purchase of food used in the food services program. Expenditures for food used in instruction in a regular classroom are recorded under object code 4300, Materials and Supplies.

5000-5999 SERVICES AND OTHER OPERATING EXPENDITURES. This classification is used for expenditures for services, rents, leases, maintenance contracts, dues, travel, insurance, utilities, and legal and other operating expenditures. These expenditures may be authorized by contracts, agreements, or purchase orders.

6000-6599 CAPITAL OUTLAY. All expenditures for the purchase of sites, buildings, and equipment are charged in this group of object codes. Books for a new or materially expanded library may also be charged here. Leases with option to purchase are also included.

- **6100 Sites and Improvement of Sites**—Some of the expenditures in this category include appraisal fees, search and title insurance, surveys, and condemnation proceedings and fees. Costs to remove buildings on newly acquired sites are also charged to this account. Preparation of sites would include grading, landscaping, seeding, and planting shrubs and trees. Also, furnishing and installing—for the first time—fixed playground apparatus, flagpoles, gateways, fences, and underground storage tanks would be identified with 6100 object codes.

- **6200 Buildings and Improvement of Buildings**—The costs of construction or purchase of new buildings as well as additions to and replacements of obsolete buildings are charged to this classification. Other expenses—including advertising, architectural and engineering fees, blueprints, and inspection services—are also recorded in this object code, as are other expenditures for buildings, include plumbing, electrical work, sprinkling, heating, and ventilating.

6300 BOOKS AND MEDIA FOR NEW SCHOOL LIBRARIES OR MAJOR EXPANSION OF SCHOOL LIBRARIES. This classification is used to record expenditures for books and materials for new and expanded libraries.

6400 EQUIPMENT. This classification is to record initial and additional purchase of items of equipment. The purchase of furniture, vehicles, machinery, motion picture film, videotape, and furnishings that are not integral parts of a building or building system would be charged to this classification.

6500 EQUIPMENT REPLACEMENT. This category is used to purchase replacement equipment. The criteria for distinguishing equipment from supplies include the following:

- the item will last more than one year
- the item needs to be replaced, rather than repaired
- the item is an independent unit, rather than incorporated into another unit
- the cost of inventory tagging the item is a small percentage of its cost
- the price exceeds some minimum dollar value established by the district.

7000-7399 OTHER OUTGO. This object code is used for all other charges and expenses incurred by the district. Charges in this classification include payments for students enrolled in state or county special schools and transfers of funds to charter schools.

SUMMARY

Program budgeting provides the board of education, staff, and community with specific costs for each program and department. The system uses account codes that identify each program in the district. For example, all charges incurred by the English department at the high school are entered against one specific account so that staff can track the specific costs each year for this particular curriculum area and site.

Careful accounting for expenditures gives a district a much clearer picture of the cost of each program and facilitates planning for the next year's budget. Proper accounting is also of great assistance in end-of-year auditing.

KEY TERMS

Account codes

Books & supplies

California School Accounting Manual

Capital outlay

Certificated salaries

Classified salaries

Employee benefits

ERMD

Fixed costs

Incremental (historical) budgeting

Object codes

PPBES

PPBS

SBB

Service & other operating expenditures

Spendable resources

ZBB

DISCUSSION/ESSAY QUESTIONS

1. The major reason for program budgeting is to provide information regarding the cost of each individual program. Give an example of one educational program for which program budgeting is utilized. Describe the types of information that could be gleaned from this process.

2. What is the most common type of program budgeting used in school districts? What are the advantages and disadvantages of this type budgeting?

3. Compare and contrast the advantages and disadvantages of PPBS and ZBB.

4. Site-Based Budgeting (SBB) is very popular in California school districts. What are the advantages and possible disadvantages of this budget system?

5. Account codes incorporate seven elements: fund/account group, resource, project year, goal, function (activity), object, and an optional field for school code. What is the meaning of an object code?

6. Accounting transactions for school district expenditures may be grouped under summary headings or listed in exhaustive detail. What are the major advantages of each approach?

7. Either the principal/program manager or the business manager may have final responsibility for designating the expenditure object code on a requisition. Which of the two administrators should have ultimate responsibility and why?

8. Object codes run in a series from 1000s to 8000s. Which group of codes would account for the largest expenditures in a district budget? What expenditures are included in that classification?

9. Textbooks and other books are charged to object codes in the 4000 series. However, books and media for new or expanded libraries are charged to the 6000 series. What is the rationale for this difference?

CHAPTER 7

SCHOOL DISTRICT REVENUE

INTRODUCTION

Although education is a function of the state, this responsibility has been delegated to local school districts. Because many local districts have trouble generating and managing their finances, states are assuming greater financial responsibility for schools. With this responsibility comes greater control over the schools.

The sales tax and personal income tax are the two major sources of revenue for states. Because states currently pay more than 50% of the cost of education, these two taxes have become key elements in the overall support of public education.

A basic question remains: How best to fund California's schools? Some educational advocates have suggested a statewide sales tax; others propose a new approach to school support from local property taxes. Still others see no need to increase the dollars flowing into school districts since states like New Jersey, which spends twice the amount per child as does California, do not produce measurably higher student achievement.

It has also been suggested that the vehicle by which funds flow to students may be flawed. Many citizens and educators believe that each school site should be empowered to collect monies directly from local taxpayers or the state. The school could use this money to purchase support from the district or the county, much as a private company might do. It has also been suggested that the school board turn most control over to local sites, meeting only two to three times per year to establish broad policies for the schools.

CURRENT FUNDING

All California school districts receive funds from state, local, and federal sources. Some of these funds are designated for specific purposes, while other monies have no strings attached. The state provides nearly 2/3 of the total monies for K-12 education, whereas the federal government provides nearly 7%; the remainder comes from local sources.

School funding has not remained static. Over the past decade, total funding for K-12 education has more than doubled from $13 billion to $29 billion. Meanwhile, California ADA increased from 4,817,000 to 6,050,895, approximately 26%, during this same period. Of course, inflation and new services mandated by state and federal law and court decisions have increased costs dramatically.

TAXES

Some form of taxation is perhaps as old as human communication. It is not too difficult to imagine the cave man demanding three animal furs for the right to share his cave with another individual. While the contribution of furs does not fit the modern definition of a tax, it has some of the essential elements.

Taxes are referred to in early historical documents included the Bible. Terms in the Old Testament refer to taxes as "assessments," "tributes," and "tolls." Taxes were first mentioned in Exodus 30:11-16, where every Jew was required to pay an annual tax. In the New Testament Jesus, when asked about paying taxes to Rome, gave the oft-quoted response, "Give to Caesar what is Caesar's, and to God what is God's" (Matthew 22:17-22). Black defines a tax as any contribution imposed by government upon individuals, for use by the government (Black, 1991).

Citizens have always had a love/hate relationship with taxes. Individuals greatly enjoy the benefits of services provided by taxes, e.g., schools, roads, police and fire protection, and health services. However, history is replete with citizens refusing to pay taxes. Often this refusal has led to civil unrest or even war, as in the case of Americans rebelling against England with the cry, "No taxation without representation."

One can almost hear the collective groans on April 15 when it is pay-up time for the national income tax or in December and April, when property taxes fall due. Perhaps the strongest support for a tax comes when the individual does not have to pay it. And yet, Americans have a good track record of supporting all levels of government by paying their taxes in general assent to Benjamin Franklin's statement that nothing is more certain than death and taxes.

CLASSIFICATION OF TAXES

Taxes are generally classified as proportional, progressive, and regressive. Proportional taxes occur when one taxpayer's percentage is the same as that of all other taxpayers, regardless of income. A progressive tax means that the percentage increases as the individual's income become higher. Finally, a regressive tax is paid if an individual with a higher income pays a lower percentage than someone with a smaller income.

- **Proportional Tax**—Suppose that three individuals earn $30,000, $40,000, and $50,000 and they pay $3,000, $4,000, and $5,000 in taxes, respectively. Each individual is paying 10% of income for taxes. That exemplifies the proportional tax. Another example is the state sales tax. The tax on clothing or other merchandise is the same percentage for everyone, regardless of income. Generally, property taxes are proportional taxes. The tax is based on the assessed value of the home and property, and all owners pay the same percentage of the value. As discussed in an earlier chapter, this is not always the case in California.

- **Progressive Tax**—If the above individuals were paying $3,000, 8,000, and $15,000, the tax would be classified as progressive. These taxpayers are assessed 10%, 20%, and 30%, respectively. Examples of a progressive tax are the state income tax in California and the national income tax. The greater one's salary, the greater the percentage of taxes.

- **Regressive Tax**—If the same individuals were paying $3,000, $2,000, and $1,000, respectively, the tax would be classified as regressive. In some instances the sales tax operates as a regressive tax, as a buyer with low income is paying proportionally higher taxes out of disposable income than a wealthier person. For example, if food and other necessities are subject to sales tax, the tax could be regressive. In an attempt to avoid this effect, California does not place sales tax on food. The structure of sales tax greatly varies from state to state.

STATE FUNDING

The state provides the major share of funding for education. This income is largely derived from state personal income tax, sales tax, and business tax. For example, in the 1997-1998 state budget, these three sources of revenue represented more than 93% of total state revenue. Personal income tax generated approximately 50%, followed by sales tax at 33%, bank and corporation taxes at 10%, and all other general fund revenue at 7%. Other state revenues come from highway use taxes, motor vehicle fees, insurance and estate taxes, liquor taxes, and horse-racing fees. Several other taxes are designated for specific purposes; these include the Driver Training Assessment Fund, tobacco tax, and state lottery (CalFacts, 2000).

CONSUMPTION TAXES

Consumption taxes are taxes based on spending, rather than income. An example of such a tax is the state sales tax. Another form of consumption tax is the value-added tax, or VAT, which is essentially a national sales tax. The U. S. does not have a VAT, although this type of taxation has received considerable discussion and attention during the past decade. A VAT is imposed at each stage of production, from obtaining the raw material to manufacturing and retail sale. The VAT is common in industrialized countries around the world.

The term "consumption tax" is most frequently used to describe excise taxes on specific goods and services. Examples include liquors, tobacco, gasoline, hotel rooms, fine jewelry, and other luxury goods. An energy tax is also based on consumption; on the average, state and federal gasoline taxes add about 37 cents to the price of a gallon of unleaded gasoline.

The advantage of a consumption tax is that a small rate can raise enormous amounts of money. An additional five-cents-per-gallon tax on gasoline would generate more than $5 billion a year in federal revenue. A second benefit of such a tax is that as the economy improves, governments automatically benefit without having to pass new taxes. Also, raising so-called "sin taxes" on items such as tobacco and alcohol is easier to sell to voters than hiking income or property taxes. Moreover, such a tax is easily and efficiently collected through existing systems: a cash register, gasoline pump, or in monthly utility bills.

About 17% of U. S. tax revenue is raised from consumption taxes, primarily sales and excise taxes. Consumption taxes are far more important to the European Community nations, which on average obtain more than 30% of total tax revenue from such taxes. For example, Italians pay taxes equivalent to $3.80 per gallon of gasoline, the French pay $3.93, and Germans shell out about $2.66 per gallon at the pump. The Japanese pay about $3.56 per gallon, and Norway has the highest gasoline price in the world at $5.00 per gallon.

A major disadvantage of a consumption tax is that it is regressive. A tax on necessities penalizes the poor and middle classes more than the rich. Estimates indicate that an energy tax would cost middle-income families four times as much of their total household income as the wealthy, while poor families would pay eight times more. A second problem is that consumption tax revenues drop as an economy slows, just when government services are needed most.

BASE REVENUE LIMIT

The major portion of each district's income is its "revenue limit," the specific amount that it may receive from state and property taxes. This amount is calculated according to a formula provided by the California Department of Education. The revenue limit for each district is multiplied by the district's actual attendance. As noted in Chapter 5, this figure is normally lower than enrollment. Since a district's state income is largely determined by attendance, accuracy of enrollment projections and programs to improve student attendance are extremely important.

Usually California's budget has included a cost-of-living adjustment (COLA) to the district's revenue limit. The COLA is intended to enable the district to keep up with inflation. Unfortunately, although the legislature approved a COLA for California school districts, it was not funded during the early 1990s. As the state economy improved, however, an average 7.9% COLA was funded each year from 1995-96 through 2000-01.

CATEGORICAL AID

In addition to the state's allocation of funds for general educational purposes, funds are also authorized for specific purposes. Categorical aid is an important part of every district's income, some coming from the federal and some from the state government. Only a relatively small portion of state allocations is directed to the 40-plus state categorical programs, whereas most federal money for schools is for special purposes or categorical programs.

Every California district receives some categorical aid. Some allocations are automatically sent to school districts; others require application. Some are based on the characteristics of the children or families in a district, such as gifted and talented, special education, non-English-speaking, low income, or migrant. Other categorical funds are directed toward specific activities or expenses; these include school improvement, urban impact aid, educational technology, mentor teachers, year-round school incentives, restructuring, home-to-school transportation, instructional materials, and child care.

LOTTERY FUNDS

The California lottery was touted to the public as a great benefit to schools. When advocates of the lottery were attempting to persuade California voters to approve its passage, television commercials showed students using computers paid for by lottery funds and students taking special field trips. However, from a high point of $179 per pupil in

1988-1989, the amount has leveled at about $100 to $120 per pupil since 1992-93 (see Figure 5 in Chapter 5).

Decline in the purchase of lottery tickets has resulted in reduced monies per pupil. The total educational income from the lottery is expected to provide between 2% and 3% of funding for school districts in 2000-01. This amount is much below that perceived by the public. In reality, lottery funds have not greatly contributed to financing of education. Because quarterly payments of lottery funds have varied widely, most business managers budget lottery income in a very conservative fashion.

An unusual and welcome sum of additional lottery income became available to schools in 2000. The original proposition stipulated that all unclaimed jackpots were to be returned to public education. Most unclaimed winnings have been small amounts. However, a $25-million jackpot went unclaimed on July 7, 2000, making it the largest unclaimed jackpot in California history. The unredeemed ticket had been purchased at a 7-Eleven market in Los Angeles. This is one case in which an unexpected windfall greatly benefitted schools, since $25 million buys 833,300 new textbooks or pays the salaries of 600 new teachers.

FEDERAL FUNDING

Federal revenue includes categorical projects such as child nutrition and vocational education. Other federal programs include the Improving America's Schools Act and impact aid (for districts whose boundaries enclose military installations). On the average, federal funding amounts to approximately 7% of the total income of a California school district. Not all districts, however, have the qualifying programs or students; therefore, federal income is unevenly divided among districts. Except for funds allocated for children living on federal land, all federal programs restrict the purposes for which the funds may be expended.

LOCAL FUNDING

Since the passage of Proposition 13, school districts largely depend upon the state for their income. In 1999-2000 approximately 35% of school district revenues were derived from local property taxes. Property taxes are the primary source of cash for local governments. Property taxes are collected on land and the buildings on it—whether they are homes, farms, industrial plants, or commercial buildings. However, this money is not collected directly by local school districts, but becomes part of the state allocation to fund education.

DEVELOPER FEES AND MELLO-ROOS DISTRICTS

Developer fees and formation of a Mello-Roos district are two avenues for obtaining funds for student housing. Developer fees are a source of revenue for school districts to partially offset the cost of building schools for the students who live in the new homes built by developers. In the year 2000 the amount chargeable per square foot was 33 cents for commercial property and $2.05 for residential construction. Developer fees and Mello-Roos fees, both of which can be used for construction or reconstruction of facilities or for portable classrooms, are more common in areas of the state where the population is increasing. Current litigation may yield a decision allowing districts that experience increasing student enrollment to collect additional fees.

CERTIFICATES OF PARTICIPATION (COPs)

Lease financing is a mechanism through which a school district may borrow money without going to voters for approval. Under this plan a district pays an annual rent on buildings that it leases from a specially created corporation. Investors in the corporation provide money up-front and receive Certificates of Participation, or COPs. The COPs specify the interest the investor is to receive. The COPs process is popular with school districts; they used this procedure to borrow $828 million, a new high, in the 1993-94 fiscal year and more recently, $442 million in 1998-99 (Connell, 1995, 2000).

GENERAL OBLIGATION BONDS (GO-BONDS)

The sale of general obligation bonds is another means of financing school construction. However, authority to issue bonds must be obtained from the voters of a school district, with 2/3, rather than just a majority, giving approval. Most districts find it very difficult to obtain so many favorable votes. In hopes of boosting the likelihood of passing school bond measures—but only after a great deal of effort—citizen groups and members of the educational establishment successfully qualified an amendment to the state constitution (Proposition 39) on the fall 2000 ballot that reduced the necessary margin for approval to 55%.

OTHER SOURCES OF INCOME

Other sources of local funds include user fees, interest income, sale and lease of property, cafeteria fees, and library fines. Districts may form partnerships with other governmental agencies to provide fee-supported programs at school sites. For example, forming a partnership with the local recreation department to provide swimming or other recreational activities is a common practice.

School districts are prohibited from charging students or their parents for books or supplies. However, after several court challenges, the California Supreme Court ruled in 1992 that a district may charge for student transportation. Still, districts may not charge for transporting special education students or for student participation in school programs such as athletics.

DONATIONS

Donations are also sources of income in many districts. Foundations and corporations frequently make grants directly to school districts for special programs. Many companies also encourage their employees to volunteer in schools.

REVENUE ACCOUNTS

The *California School Accounting Manual* (2000) requires all district revenues to be identified with 8000 series object codes. Districts have a large number of revenue sources, and each source must be accounted for by a separate ledger number. This accounting procedure enables the school board, administration, teachers, and the public to track each income source. The state manual contains an example of a district's revenue section of the General Fund budget; see Figure 6.

Figure 6

**Sample of District Income
with Revenue Object Codes**

Revenue Code	Source of Income	Amount
8010-8099	Revenue Limit Sources	
8011	Principal Apportionment/State Aid—Current Year	$ 277,528
8041	Secured Roll Taxes	345,888
8042	Unsecured Roll Taxes	2,700
8100-8299	Federal Revenue	
8110	Maintenance and Operations	2,500
8170	Job Training Partnership Act	1,000
8300-8599	Other State Revenue	
8331	Gifted and Talented Pupils	1,148
8342	Home-to-School Transportation	7,500
8600-8799	Other Local Revenues	
8799	Other Transfers in/from All Others	3,000
	Total Estimated Revenue	$ 641,264

Source: *California School Accounting Manual.* (2000).

SUMMARY

Even the most severe critic of public education would agree that California schools are facing a difficult period. In addition to the continuing recession in California with concurrent reduction in state resources, student population continues to increase, placing a greater burden on the taxpayer. It had been estimated that student population would continue to increase by 150,000 students per year, a factor that would place a strain on the budget just to build or renovate facilities. However, as previously pointed out, enrollment growth, although still under way, slowed to less than 100,000 annually in 1995-96. Clearly, long-term enrollment projections need to be monitored carefully.

In addition to coping with the increase in student enrollment, many districts are channeling scarce resources into programs for new immigrants to California who are limited in English proficiency. Other districts are attempting to cope with gangs and student discipline by employing additional security guards to ensure a safe environment for students.

Local school districts are largely dependent on the state for income, with 2/3 of their revenue coming from that source. Districts are exploring a variety of options to provide additional revenue, such as charging fees for services and various attempts to obtain funds for school construction. Restructuring the delivery of education and development of charter schools, with more financial autonomy at the site level, are under discussion as possible ways to reduce costs. It is likely that these possibilities and others will be implemented in this decade in the endeavor to maintain a system of free public education in California.

KEY TERMS

ADA

Business tax

COLA

Consumption tax

COPs

Developer fees

GO-bonds

Improving America's Schools Act (IASA)

Income tax

Mello-Roos

Partnerships

Progressive tax

Property tax

Regressive tax

Revenue accounts

Sales tax

Sin tax

Title I, Title II, etc.

User fees

Value-added tax

DISCUSSION/ESSAY QUESTIONS

1. The three major sources of revenue for California school districts are the state income tax, state sales tax, and property tax. What are the advantages and disadvantages of each of these sources of government income?

2. The United States does not currently have a value-added tax (VAT). What are the major arguments for and against this form of taxation?

3. "Sin taxes" are increasingly popular with federal and state legislatures. Give an example of a "sin tax" and discuss the pros and cons of this form of taxation.

4. Nearly all federal monies allocated for public education are "categorical." Explain this term and give examples of federal categorical aid to school districts. What is the rationale for each?

5. Briefly, discuss the revenue sources for school construction and the advantages and disadvantages of each.

CHAPTER 8

SCHOOL DISTRICT FUNDS

INTRODUCTION

California school districts use an accounting system known as "fund accounting." This system is also used by other government entities. Hartman (1988) defined a fund as

> an independent accounting entity that has a self-balancing set of accounts. The accounts are designed to record all financial resources, assets, liabilities, encumbrances, and equities that are recorded for attaining certain objectives. Assets, liabilities, and encumbrances are all included within a particular fund to carry on a specific district activity.

The largest and most active fund is the General Fund. This is the fund in which all the accounts that directly support the educational program are contained. For example, salaries, fringe benefits, textbooks, and instructional supplies are contained in the General Fund. Each fund has a separate ending balance that may be divided into restricted and unrestricted accounts. A restricted account may be expended only for certain purposes, while an unrestricted account may be used for any general purpose within the guidelines established for the fund.

Most school districts operate with as few funds as necessary to maintain a cost-efficient system, keeping staff and auditing time to a minimum. Auditors typically audit each fund separately. The object codes that make up each fund are the same for all funds. For example, the 6400 account (equipment) has the same object code and name in the building fund as it has in the general fund.

PUBLIC SCHOOL ACCOUNTING

Public school accounting requires separate accounting systems for each fund. Accounting for these funds is the basis for the auditors' annual report. In their report, auditors list both income and expenditure accounts and amounts. Table 4 lists the funds utilized by schools in California. Note that some funds are more restricted than others as to how monies may be expended.

CLASSIFICATION AND TYPES OF FUNDS

The Governmental Accounting Standards Board, the National Center for Educational Statistics, and the Association of School Business Officials recommend four major fund classifications, with separate funds in each. The four classifications are

- Governmental Funds
- Proprietary Funds
- Fiduciary Funds
- Account Groups.

Governmental Funds are divided in turn into the General Fund, Special Revenue Fund, Capital Project Fund, and Debt Service Fund. Proprietary Funds are divided into Enterprise Funds and Internal Service Funds. Fiduciary Funds include the Trust and Agency Fund and Account Groups contain general fixed assets and general long-term debt.

GOVERNMENTAL FUNDS

GENERAL FUND. The General Fund is the most common type; it is utilized by every school district. All financial resources are accounted for in this fund, which is used to account for the ordinary operations of the district. Only those transactions required by law to be handled in another fund are omitted from the General Fund.

SPECIAL REVENUE FUND. Special Revenue Funds are established to account for the proceeds from specific revenue sources restricted to paying for specified activities or programs. For example, the Adult Education Fund is used to account separately for federal, state, and local revenues for adult education programs. The Cafeteria Fund is used to account separately for federal, state, and local revenue to operate the food service program. Other special revenue funds include the Child Development and Deferred Maintenance Funds.

Table 4

California School Districts
Types of Funds

General Fund
This is the primary fund for all school district operations. This fund includes both restricted and unrestricted school district revenue and expenditures.

Bond Interest and Redemption Fund (restricted)
These monies are property tax collections used to pay bonded indebtedness.

Building Fund
This fund is for capital improvements. Bond issue receipts and monies from sales of lands are deposited in this account. Building improvements and buses may be purchased from the Building Fund.

Special Reserve Fund
This account may be used for any purpose a board of education designates.

State School Lease-Purchase Fund (restricted)
This fund is used much like the Building Fund.

Cafeteria Fund (or Account) (restricted)
The labor and operational costs for Food Services are included in this fund.

Child Development Fund (restricted)
All funds related to the district Child Development Program are deposited in this fund.

Adult Education Fund (restricted)
This fund is directed to the district's Adult Education Program.

Other
This category may be used for self-insurance reserve.

Deferred Maintenance Fund (restricted)
This account is used for school and district maintenance projects and is partially supported by the state.

Capital Facilities Fund (restricted)
Developers' fees are deposited in and expended from this fund. These are fees collected from builders of new housing to provide schools for the children who will live in the homes.

Pupil Transportation Equipment Fund (restricted)
Funds from this account purchase school buses and other equipment for transporting students.

CAPITAL PROJECTS FUNDS. Capital Projects Funds are established to account for monies for acquisition or construction of major capital facilities. They are maintained for each capital project in the district. Capital projects usually involve acquiring or building major capital facilities such as land, buildings, or equipment.

DEBT SERVICE FUNDS. Debt Service Funds account for the accumulation of resources for, and the payment of, principal and interest on long-term debt. There are three types of Debt Service Funds: Bond Interest and Redemption Fund, Tax Override Fund, and Debt Service Fund.

School districts typically finance their capital expenditures by selling bonds. A Debt Service Fund is created so that when bond payments are due, funds are available for this expenditure. Proceeds from the sale of bonds are deposited in the county treasury. Any premiums or accrued interest received from the sale of the bonds must be deposited in the Bond Interest and Redemption Fund of the district.

The county auditor maintains control of the district's Bond Interest and Redemption Fund. Principal and interest on the bonds must be paid by the county treasurer from taxes levied by the county auditor-controller.

PROPRIETARY FUNDS

Proprietary Funds are similar to those used in private industry. Revenue deposited in these accounts comes from such sources as charges for services. Proprietary Funds are divided into two separate parts: Enterprise Funds and the Internal Service Fund.

ENTERPRISE FUNDS. In some cases, fees are charged for services or merchandise. Examples are funds established by a bookstore, the yearbook, school newspaper, or athletics. Enterprise funds may be used for operations that meet either of two conditions:

- The fund is financed and operated in a manner similar to that employed by private enterprises. The cost of goods or services can be financed and recovered from charges to users.

- The board has determined that revenues earned or expenses incurred are appropriate for capital maintenance, management control, or accountability. For example, the Cafeteria Fund may be recorded as an enterprise fund, rather than a special reserve fund.

INTERNAL SERVICE FUND. Sometimes one department in a school district may perform a service for another department. For example, the printing department typically services several other operations. Similarly, many departments requisition merchandise from the district warehouse. Costs for these internal service centers are documented in Internal Service Funds.

FIDUCIARY FUNDS

"Fiduciary" pertains to a trustee or guardian or a person who holds a thing in trust. This fund is used when the district serves as an intermediary in the distribution of funds. The procedure is similar to that of an attorney serving as executor of an estate. To keep track of deposits and expenditures of these monies, a fiduciary fund is established. There are usually two parts to the Fiduciary Fund, one for trust funds and the other for agency funds.

TRUST FUNDS. The district serves as the agent in disbursing monies from Trust Funds. An example is establishment of a fund to continue to pay retirement benefits to employees.

AGENCY FUND. Examples of Agency Funds include student body monies and the treasuries of teacher and parent organizations. Sources of receipts include fund-raising ventures; student store merchandise; athletic events and student body performances; and income from concessions, publications, and gifts.

ACCOUNT GROUPS

In addition to the funds, two account groups are used in fund accounting; they are the General Fixed-Asset Account Group and the General Long-Term Account Group. The account groups are self-balancing sets of accounting records that track the existence and amounts of the general fixed assets and the general long-term debt of the district. The term "general" in the title of the account groups indicates that the assets and long-term debt are not included in specific funds. It is important to keep these monies separate from the current operation of the district.

GENERAL FIXED-ASSET ACCOUNT GROUP. The General Fixed-Asset Account Group permits management control and accountability by listing the district's fixed assets. General fixed assets are district-owned assets of a physical nature that are expected to remain useful for a long period of time. They include equipment, machinery, buildings, and building improvements. Education Code Section 35168 requires a district to maintain information on each piece of equipment, including name, description, cost, identification number, acquisition date, location, and the time and means of disposal.

Districts should maintain similar information for all fixed assets. The records for fixed assets should include actual cost. If actual cost is unknown, the district should make an estimate. Cost of donated fixed assets should be recorded as the estimated fair market value at the time received.

GENERAL LONG-TERM DEBT ACCOUNT GROUP. The General Long-Term Debt Account Group is established to account for the unmatured principal of long-term indebtedness that is not the primary obligation of the proprietary or trust funds. Long-term debt is composed of outstanding bonds, long-term notes payable, long-term leases, and long-term liabilities for compensated absence. Typically, long-term debts are incurred to construct or purchase buildings, land, and equipment.

Other examples of long-term debts include legal judgments and unfunded pension liabilities. The district should maintain detailed information on all long-term debts, including issue dates, interest rates, total debts outstanding, and principal and interest payments.

SUMMARY

To simplify the procedure of collecting and disbursing resources, districts utilize the governmental fund concept. For example, in the Adult Education Fund, income is collected into specific income accounts and disbursed through expenditures accounts—all activity occurring within the fund. A fund is used to meet a specific objective, in this case, support of all adult education activities within the school district.

Most school districts operate with as few funds as necessary to maintain a cost-efficient system. The use of separate funds ensures that revenues and expenditures set aside for specific purposes are not commingled and provides districts with an efficient and accurate accounting procedure. Utilization of this concept also assists the district's auditor in his or her task.

KEY TERMS

Account groups
Adult Education Fund
Bond Interest & Redemption Fund
Building Fund
Cafeteria Fund (Account)
Capital Facilities Fund
Child Development Fund
Debt Service Fund
Deferred Maintenance Fund

Fiduciary Funds
Fixed assets
Fund accounting
General Fund
Government Funds
Proprietary Funds
Pupil Transportation Fund
Special Reserve Fund
State School Lease Purchase Fund

DISCUSSION/ESSAY QUESTIONS

1. School districts are required to establish a separate fund for several categories of income and expenditures. Describe fund accounting and give the reasons for this accounting procedure.

2. Most California school districts have four different classifications of funds. Name the four types and give a brief description of each classification.

3. The terms "restricted" and "unrestricted" are used to describe the various funds. Explain the meaning of "restricted fund" and give an example.

4. A Debt Service Fund may be used by California school districts. What is the purpose of this type of fund? Give an example of monies that could be collected and spent in this classification.

5. California school district auditors often find improper procedures, sometimes no procedures at all, for managing a district's general fixed assets. Explain the term "fixed assets," describe procedures that meet legal requirements, and give reasons why auditors often find fault with districts in this regard.

CHAPTER 9

SCHOOL SITE BUDGETING

INTRODUCTION

Over the past several years more than a third of the nation's schools have adopted some form of site-based management. This trend is driven by the belief that school districts need to disperse and deregulate the power and authority of the central office (Mitchell & Treiman, 1993). Those who advocate shifting managerial control from central offices to school sites believe that individual schools can make better educational decisions for the students at that site.

The success of the total educational program at any individual school depends on effective leadership in fiscal planning. A principal cannot function as an effective instructional leader unless she is knowledgeable of financial management. As leaders, principals focus on making a school function well for both staff and students. Teachers, support staff, and students must be provided with the necessary equipment, books, and supplies to be effective. The school plant must be maintained as a safe, attractive and comfortable place for students and employees. To accomplish these objectives, the principal must be skilled in planning and developing the budget and in interpreting it to the superintendent, school board, and community.

Site-based budgeting involves decentralization of power in a district and requires that the superintendent and governing board relinquish some of their control over the ways in which funds are spent. This decision is a difficult hurdle in some districts. Allocating a "lump sum" portion of the district budget to a school site is risky and requires a foundation of trust on the part of the superintendent and board as well as a commitment to acquire new skills on the part of site administration and staff.

Developing, monitoring, and accounting for the school site budget is a major responsibility of the principal. In most districts, the school principal is responsible for maintaining and monitoring the budget at the school site. A school budget is a planning document that links educational policy to financial decisions. It contains a school's priorities and serves as a blueprint, or road map, for meeting the objectives of the school. Decisions typically made by the principal and staff include the level of financial support for library and media services, instructional technology, school athletics, music and art programs, and cafeteria services. Hundreds of financial decisions define the priorities of the school and the district.

The degree of site-level responsibility for the school budget varies greatly from district to district. Because of the constraints imposed by district staffing formulas, labor contracts, and provisions of California's Education Code, a principal may have limited discretion as to certificated and classified staffing. In fact, in some districts very few expenditure categories fall under a principal's authority. Even in the most centralized districts, however, a principal usually has some control over the purchase of instructional, office, and custodial supplies, field trips, and conference attendance, with more limited authority over purchase of textbooks and capital outlay equipment.

Other districts, by contrast, may have decentralized many budget decisions to the site level, including management of utility bills, maintenance costs, and capital outlay. In such a district, personnel decisions may also be highly decentralized. For example, a principal may have the authority to increase class size so as to employ a reading resource teacher or an art specialist instead of a classroom teacher. Financial decision-making can be expected to devolve more to the site level as the move toward site-based management, as exemplified in the LEARN proposal in the Los Angeles Unified School District, gains momentum.

BUDGET WORKSHEET

After educational and budget priorities have been established, the principal develops a preliminary budget worksheet. The worksheet is used by the district office to establish school accounts for the next school year. The worksheet for Hesperia Unified School District (Figure 7) is presented as typical of those required by many California districts.

Figure 7

Example of a Site Level Worksheet

HESPERIA UNIFIED SCHOOL DISTRICT
2001-2002 PRELIMINARY BUDGET WORKSHEET

1000 ACCOUNTS—CERTIFICATED SALARIES

1110	$_____	Contract Salaries
1140	$_____	Substitute Salaries
1150	$_____	Teacher Salaries—Other Pay (Stipends)
1230	$_____	Counselor Salaries
1310	$_____	Administrator/Director/Coordinator Salaries

3000 ACCOUNTS—CERTIFICATED BENEFITS

Benefits must be budgeted. Multiply the totals above by each of the percentages listed for the account. Note that benefit percentages may change.

3331	$_____	Medicare (1.45%)
3501	$_____	Unemployment Insurance (0.13%)
3601	$_____	Workers' Comp (1.94%)
3101	$_____	STRS (8.25%)
3411	$_____	Health and Welfare ($567 per month per person)

2000 ACCOUNTS—CLASSIFIED SALARIES

2110	$_____	Instructional Aide Salaries
2210	$_____	Classified Support Salaries
2310	$_____	Classified Supervisors & Administrators
2410	$_____	Clerical & Office Salaries

3000 ACCOUNTS—CLASSIFIED BENEFITS

Benefits for Part-time Employees (Less than 4 hours)

3332 $_____ Medicare (1.45%)
3350 $_____ Alternative Retirement System Benefits (ARS)
3502 $_____ Unemployment Insurance (0.13%)
3602 $_____ Workers' Comp (1.94%)

Benefits for Classified Employees (Four hours or more)

3312 $_____ FICA (6.20%)
3332 $_____ Medicare (1.45%)
3412 $_____ Health &Welfare Benefits ($611/month per person)
3502 $_____ Unemployment Insurance (0.13%)
3602 $_____ Workers' Comp (1.94%)

4000 ACCOUNTS—BOOKS AND SUPPLIES
(Consumable Single Items Costing Less than $500)

4110 $_____ Textbooks
4210 $_____ Other Books
4210 $_____ Other Computerized Books
4310 $_____ Instructional Materials
      (Vendors/Warehouse, Testing Materials)
4330 $_____ Meeting Refreshments (Snacks, not Meals)
4340 $_____ Computer Software
4350 $_____ Office Supplies
4390 $_____ Other Supplies (Includes Computers)

5000 ACCOUNTS—Services and Operations

5200 $_____ Conference Registration
5300 $_____ Dues & Memberships
5610 $_____ Rentals & Leases
5630 $_____ Vendor Repair/Maintenance Agreement
5713 $_____ Field Trips

5714	$_____	Print Shop
5715	$_____	Postage
5810	$_____	Contracted Service
5840	$_____	Computer/Tech Related Services
		(On-Line Services/Site License)
5850	$_____	Professional/Consulting Services
5910	$_____	Communications (Telephone, Cell Phone, Pager)
5940	$_____	Internet Provider

6000 ACCOUNTS—Capitalized and Inventoried
(Single Items Costing $5,000 and up)

6150	$_____	Site Construction (Landscape/Parking Lot/Sidewalks)
6190	$_____	Other Costs—New Site Purchases
6240	$_____	Building Improvement for Technology
6250	$_____	Building Improvement/Construction
6400	$_____	Equipment
6440	$_____	Software Purchases
6450	$_____	Computers & Other Computer Hardware
6500	$_____	Equipment Replacement
6540	$_____	Software Replacement
6550	$_____	Computer-Related Hardware Replacement

SCHOOL SITE ACCOUNTING

The school budget may be handwritten on ledger sheets, entered into a school computer, or managed by direct connection to the district's data processing center. Regardless of the system used, it is important that the principal maintain a very close relationship with the district accounting department to ensure that the school budget is accurate and up-to-date.

Site budgets usually contain a four-digit object-of-expenditure code, which correlates with the district budget. Expenditure codes may take several forms. Most formats contain a goal code, a function code, and an object code. The budget document also should set out columns for original appropriation, encumbrances, amount expended, and balance.

In the sample site budget in Figure 8, the object code 1110 indicates a certificated salary appropriation.

When an order is originally placed, this amount is recorded in the encumbrance column; when the order is received and paid, this amount is placed in the expended column and—if there is a change—an adjustment made to the balance. With inflation and increases in cost of shipping, the actual bill is often greater than the originally expected cost. Unless this difference is carefully recorded, the budget may be overspent.

Although most principals delegate the day-to-day responsibilities for maintaining the site budget to a secretary or clerk, a site administrator should frequently check encumbrances and balances to ensure proper accounting. It is particularly important to check the actual cost of books, supplies, and capital outlay against the original invoice.

Figure 8

Example of a Site Level Budget

**ROUND TREE ELEMENTARY SCHOOL
2001-2002 BUDGET**

Goal	Function	Object	Appropriation	Encumbered	Expended	Balance
1110	1000	1110	$ 500.00	$ .00	$ .00	500.00
1110	1000	2110	450.00	.00	.00	450.00
1110	1000	4110	1000.00	65.00	.00	935.00
1110	1000	4310	1750.00	438.74	1165.58	145.68
1110	1000	5490	1000.00	800.00	200.00	0.00

USING EXCEL TO BUILD AND MONITOR THE SCHOOL SITE BUDGET

A school principal may request assistance from the business office for tools to ease the tasks of building and monitoring the budget. Many financial tasks can be completed more quickly and easily with a personal computer. Some of these tasks include:

- setting up the student body fund
- organizing the site level budget
- maintaining a database of school site personnel.

In several counties, districts are, in turn, provided with software to project the impact of salary increases and rising costs of fringe benefits, utilities, and other expenditure categories. Such software is also available from commercial firms. With the spread of site-based management, such software may also be useful for administrators at the site level.

This section outlines a task—setting up a school site budget—that can be performed with a software program, Excel, on a Macintosh or PC. The school decision-maker is wise to purchase a handbook for the Excel program and refer to it often. This spreadsheet program is extremely user-friendly and is mastered with little time or trouble. Figure 9 shows a typical school site spreadsheet, including the appropriation, encumbrance, and balance for each account.

Figure 9

Elements of the Spreadsheet

	A	B	C	D	E	F	G
1	Goal	Function	Object	Appropriation	Encumbered	Expended	Balance
2	1110	1000	1110	$500.00	.00	.00	$500.00
3	1110	1000	2110	$450.00	.00	.00	$450.00
4	1110	1000	4110	$1000.00	$65.00	.00	$935.00
5	1110	1000	4310	$1750.00	$438.74	$1165.58	$145.68
6	1110	1000	5940	$1000.00	$800.00	$200.00	.00

SETTING UP THE WORKSHEET. Excel conveniently sets up a worksheet, or spreadsheet, with which to develop the budget. A user types the necessary information into each "cell." The worksheet is composed of these cells, each of which is labeled with a letter representing the column (running vertically) and a number representing the row (running horizontally). Thus, the cell in the first column of the first row is cell A1, and so on.

THE HELP MENU. A user who has difficulty entering data or performing other functions may consult the excellent Help menu within the program. One scans words and phrases that are underlined on the menu, selects one of these phrases, and clicks on it with the mouse. Clicking a term underlined with a solid line jumps to a new position in the help file discussing that term. Clicking a term underlined with a dotted line pops up a small dialog box defining the topic.

USING EXCEL FUNCTIONS. Excel offers many shortcuts. The following example shows how to perform a subtraction function. Looking at Figure 9, suppose we want to subtract the numbers in cells E4 and F4 from that in cell D4 to obtain a balance in G4. The formula we would type for cell G4 is as follows:

=D4-(E4+F4)

This formula gives the balance of $935.00, as indicated in the figure. Such a formula can be copied to other cells in the same column; the formula automatically adjusts itself so that it computes a balance for each row using data in that row.

Functions available in Excel include the following:

Function	Example
Sum	=SUM(W1:W10)
Average	=AVERAGE(X10:X20)
Max	=MAX(Y1:Y10)
Min	=MIN(Z20:Z45)

THE ADVANTAGES OF EXCEL. The advantages of Excel are that you can

- create tables of data
- use formulas to calculate new information from data
- produce colorful charts based on the data
- save the work so that each month the spreadsheet can simply be updated, rather than re-created.

ORGANIZING THE SITE LEVEL BUDGET

To set up a site budget, column A may be used to list expenditure titles and Column B to list dollar amounts, as shown in Figure 10. The budget may be decreased or increased by a percentage amount. The salaries of personnel may be entered in exactly the same way. Column A may be used to list the names of the personnel and column B to list their salaries. Spreadsheet programs such as Excel easily compute simple percentages and may save the financial decision-maker much time.

SUMMARY

Almost all leadership positions in public schools require the management of public funds. Individuals seeking leadership positions in public schools should have a sound foundation in basic budgeting principles and policies. School administrators should understand the accounting system, including the way financial information is recorded, organized, and presented. The principal who provides strong financial leadership at a school site also has a strong advantage in developing an outstanding instructional program, since no instructional program can survive without needed resources. The business side of the principalship must be mastered if the instructional program is to be successful.

With the current movement toward educational restructuring and decentralized decision-making, far greater control over the budget is placed at school sites. This responsibility calls for additional training for the school administrator and support staff to ensure proper decision-making and accounting for school expenditures.

Figure 10

Site Level Budget

	A	B
1	Books and supplies	$ 400.00
2	Paper supplies	200.00
3	Equipment	200.00
4	Total	$ 800.00

KEY TERMS

Cells & addresses
Centralized district
Decentralized district
Encumbrance
Fiscal planning
Function code

Goal code
Ledger sheets
Object code
School budget
Spreadsheet

DISCUSSION/ESSAY QUESTIONS

1. The success of the total educational program at any individual school depends on effective leadership in fiscal planning. Do you agree or disagree with this statement? Support your answer with specific examples.

2. Principals are being given greater and greater responsibility for developing a budget at the school site. What are the advantages and disadvantages of this trend?

3. The school budget may be developed primarily at the district ("centralized budgeting") or at each school site ("decentralized"). What are the advantages and disadvantages of centralized budgeting?

4. An accounting procedure referred to as an "encumbrance" is widely used by school districts. What does this term mean? Why is it important?

CHAPTER 10

THE ANNUAL AUDIT

INTRODUCTION

Today's the day! The auditors will be here at 9:00 a.m. Energy is running high in the business office, and tension is building. Accounting books are stacked in the conference room; tables and desks are cleared; and the coffee is hot. What will they ask for first? This scene could describe any school district office at the onset of the annual audit.

The annual audit, a requirement of the California Education Code, can be viewed in different ways. It may be seen as positive tool—or with the feeling "They are out to get us." These perspectives vary from district to district and among personnel within a district. For a district employee who takes pride in his or her work, an audit may become a source of accolades—or of anxiety.

REQUIRED AUDIT

Each California superintendent is required by Section 41020 of the Education Code to arrange for an annual audit of all school district funds. This section states, "It is the intent of the Legislature to encourage sound fiscal management practices among school districts for the most efficient and effective use of public funds for the education of children in California by strengthening fiscal accountability at the district, county, and state levels."

Audits must be conducted by an unbiased, independent firm. Only licensed Certified Public Accountants (CPAs) or Public Accountants (PAs) are eligible to perform the audit. This independent audit gives credibility to the district report of its financial condition. The annual audit provides assurances that the information shown in the district's financial report is correct, and that no major errors or omissions exist.

The purpose of the annual audit is to provide the governing board and other interested parties with key financial information about the district from an independent perspective. A successful audit adds credibility to the district's financial statements in the eyes of creditors, bankers, investors, and others for whom it is essential to view the financial statements with confidence.

Even if an annual audit were not mandated, good management practices would require it. Each district must contract for its annual audit by April 1. If this task is not completed by the district, the county superintendent must arrange for the audit on the district's behalf. Typically, auditors work with school personnel for many months prior to November, by which time the audit must have been completed. Each district must have its audit for the previous fiscal year completed and filed with the county superintendent by December 15. If the deadline is not met, the county superintendent may grant an extension, contract with another auditor, or request the state controller to investigate the situation (Education Code sections 41020 and 41020.2). In the 1999-2000 year, 88% of the audits were filed by the December 15 date (Connell, 2000).

FEES FOR THE AUDIT

Fees for the audit are paid by the school district and vary with the size of the district and its geographic location. An audit costs more in smaller districts—those under 5,000 ADA—than in districts with higher enrollments. In 1999 the statewide average costs ranged from less than $2.00 per ADA in districts with 10,000 pupils or more to approximately $15.00 per ADA in districts with 5,000 enrollment or less (Connell, 2000).

AUDIT GUIDELINES

In 1984-1985 the state controller assumed fiscal oversight responsibilities for California school districts. To implement this responsibility, the controller

- prepares and updates an audit guide used by CPAs and PAs in conducting the annual audit

- reviews the CPA or PA audit work-papers to determine if the work performed meets the auditing and reporting requirements

- reviews each district's annual report and notifies the district and its auditor of the report's completeness and compliance with reporting guidelines

- performs follow-up reviews of specific programs and issues as required.

The California Department of Education assists the controller in preparing the audit guide that is used to ensure compliance with each year's audit. The audit guide, which fills a four-inch notebook, is updated continually. As legislation is enacted or new programs authorized by the federal and state governments, the Department of Education reviews the legislation or programs to determine if there are any compliance issues that should be included in the annual audit. These issues are then drawn to the attention of the controller, who has final responsibility for preparing the audit guide. The audit guidelines are disseminated to all certified accounting firms that perform school audits. The audits are due in the Controller's Office on November 15 of each year.

OBJECTIVES OF THE AUDIT

The best sources of information about all fund balances are the annual audited financial statements. In these documents, the audit confirms the amounts of the fund balances as well as their distribution among restricted and unrestricted funds. The objectives of the annual audit are to determine:

- if the district's financial statements provide a fair and reasonably complete picture of its financial position and activities

- if there is effective control over and a proper accounting for revenues, expenditures, assets, and liabilities

- if reports and claims to state and federal programs contain accurate and reliable data

- if state and federal funds have been spent in accordance with the terms and regulations of these programs.

The annual audit is not designed to uncover every small error, irregularity, or omission, but to find any major or consistent problems.

AUDIT PROCEDURES

In the early years of auditing, auditors thoroughly examined all district financial transactions. About 1900, as-large scale business enterprises developed, auditors began to use sampling techniques in the auditing process. Since then, not every payroll warrant or purchase order is checked. The purpose of the audit is to ensure that all documents represent fairly the financial condition of the district. The audit provides an independent assessment of the accounting controls of the district.

Auditors are responsible for examining the district's bookkeeping and accounting procedures to uncover waste, fraud, and inefficiency. Auditors are also concerned with proper accounting procedures to ensure accuracy and reliability of accounting data. Since the vast share of district funds is allocated to personnel, auditors pay special attention to position control—the allocation, employment, and replacement of personnel in each program. A mechanism should be developed in every district to ensure that personnel allocations are not exceeded without prior approval.

Any factors that might materially affect the financial condition of the district are noted in the audit report. For example, if a lawsuit might affect the district negatively, this is noted as a possible liability.

ASSEMBLY BILL 1200

As a result of bankruptcy, or near bankruptcy, of several California school districts, Assembly Bill 1200 was approved by the state legislature in 1991. The key concept of this legislation required that a district's budget meet financial obligations in the current fiscal year as well as multi-year financial commitments. Assembly Bill 1708, approved in 1993, clarified the term "multi-year." The district's budget must show solvency in both the current year and the next succeeding fiscal years.

With implementation of these laws, school audits have become more than just a routine procedure, and much greater attention has been given to the audit process. Assembly Bill 1200 increased the authority of the county superintendent of schools and the State Superintendent of Public Instruction over a school district's financial matters. According to Brittan (1992), this legislation has become the focal point of the auditing process. It has given county superintendents greater authority to intervene when warning signs of financial difficulty are observed in a district.

Melendez (1991), Director of Research and Policy Analysis for the Association of California School Administrators, suggests that this legislation requires greater financial expertise on the part of school superintendents. No longer can the superintendent delegate total responsibility for managing the district's financial affairs to the business manager. If a district's financial house is not in order, blame will be placed on the superintendent for not anticipating a budget shortfall or for implementing expensive employee contracts or programs without adequate resources to pay the bills.

GENERAL FUND

The auditor is required to review the General Fund of the district, as well as individual funds such as student body and cafeteria accounts. The General Fund is the primary focus of the school district audit. The expenditures and income that the district actually received and spent are compared against budgeted amounts. The audit report notes significant differences in the amounts budgeted and actual revenue or expenditures. This information provides a guideline for future budgeting.

The net ending balance is of special interest to the school board, superintendent, and staff. This calculation shows the amount of money that the district has at the end of the fiscal year. It is called the district's savings or reserve. If the ending balance is over or under estimates, the business manager must determine why this situation occurred.

STUDENT BODY FUND

Auditors spend much of their time analyzing student body accounts. They examine whether expenditures were correctly approved by the student body officers and the authorized administrator. High school student body accounts are especially complicated, since food and athletic sales account for much of the activity.

AUDITOR'S OPINION

Upon completion of the annual audit, the district may receive any one of three types of auditor opinions regarding the district's management and accounting practices.

UNQUALIFIED OPINION. An unqualified opinion means that no significant deviations from generally accepted accounting practices (GAAP) were noted. Scott (1990), an employee of the auditing firm of Vavrinek, Trine, Day, and Company, sets forth several guidelines for an unqualified opinion:

- The district must have competent employees with experience and education in the specific business area of their assignment.

- The district must have in place an internal orientation and training program designed to familiarize employees with school business.

- There should be a business services handbook with detailed policies and procedures.

- Competent auditors should be selected who have the skill, experience, and time commitment to perform the audit in a complete and competent fashion.

QUALIFIED OPINION. A qualified opinion indicates some problem with the financial records of the district. For example, attendance records at the high school may not be kept according to state guidelines. This example may cause the district to experience a loss of funds from the state. Another audit exception might be found in funds of the student body organization in a high school. Unless these are monitored carefully, expenditures or income may not be accounted for correctly.

The most common deviation in California school districts is accounting for fixed assets. Because maintaining the inventory of fixed assets requires extensive personnel time and cost, districts frequently fail to maintain these records according to accepted accounting principles.

NO OPINION. If the auditor reports "no opinion," district records are so poor, or even nonexistent, that the auditors cannot form any opinion at all about the financial status of the school district. Consequently, the audit may be delayed until records can be reconstructed—or the auditor may assign a "No Opinion" status.

In the 1999-2000 fiscal year there were 16 qualified and three negative or no opinion audit reports. This number was slightly higher than in 1998-1999, when 15 qualified or negative opinions were filed (Connell, 2000).

VALUE OF THE AUDIT REPORT

The audit report is used by the district superintendent, school board, and county superintendent as an independent review of the financial condition of the district. The report may also contain recommendations to improve procedures and increase efficiency in the business functions of the district. The report is useful to state and federal agencies that fund particular programs in the district. Business and commercial agencies also review the report when considering loan extensions or new credit for the district.

MANAGEMENT RECOMMENDATIONS

Frequently, the audit contains management recommendations indicating ways in which recordkeeping could be improved. Recommendations made by the auditor can strengthen and streamline the district's internal controls, as well as its accounting and administrative practices. Implementing these recommendations may help the district cut costs in its operations and ensure that existing resources are used in an efficient and economical manner. Ordinarily, the business staff takes steps during the year to address each of the auditor's recommendations so they do not reappear in subsequent audit reports.

AUDIT COMMITTEE

Over the years many school districts have formed a special Audit Committee to enhance fiscal accountability. Audits cost school districts a significant sum of money and staff time. The work of an Audit Committee can reduce these costs and serve as an added safeguard to ensure prudent supervision of a district's finances. An Audit Committee provides a useful service to the district by promoting communication between the auditor on the one hand, and the school board and administration on the other. Many districts have found that audit committees improve quality and spread knowledge of financial reporting.

The objectives of an ongoing independent audit committee received additional attention in California in 1991-1992, when a financial officer in Newport-Mesa Unified School District was accused of stealing more than $3 million. This district was meeting all legal audit requirements; however, the district had not attended to suggested improvements in accounting offered by its auditor.

Audit committees should include people who have experience with financial management and the audit process. The work of the committee focuses additional attention on the audit function and can relieve anxiety among community members by showing that prudent measures have been established to safeguard taxpayers' monies.

The audit committee should include members of the business staff, as well as board members and the chief business officer. It is also prudent to include other community members with expertise in accounting and finance. A local certified public accountant, a banker, or a financial advisor, for example, could introduce an outside, unbiased check on a district's internal controls.

The purposes of the committee should be well defined by board policy or administrative regulation. Some responsibilities of this committee might include reviewing procedures for handling voided checks, security of blank checks, and signature requirements for checks. The committee could also spot-check bills paid and payroll checks issued. Although an internal audit committee is unlikely to identify serious problems, the existence of such a committee tends to make the staff more careful about following procedures and might reduce temptation among some employees to take advantage of the system. It could also reassure school boards and members of the community that public funds are well managed and that proper controls are in place.

An audit committee can be helpful in discussing implementation of management recommendations with the auditors. Effecting all the audit recommendations may be impossible in times of financial constraints. In such situations a multi-year plan might yield necessary controls without further financial distress to the district.

If an extremely complicated issue arises, a district may contract with an auditor to perform an *ad hoc* analysis of the budget. In this situation, the auditing firm may report directly to the board of education. If legal or personnel issues are involved, the report may be presented in closed session.

SUMMARY

Over the last decade, managing financial resources of schools has become an increasingly difficult task. All California school districts are required to complete an annual audit. The audit is an important resource for school boards, administration, and the community. It provides information on the district's financial position, on compliance with various laws and regulations, and on adherence to good management practices. Most important, this information is gathered through independent review by a professional accountant specifically trained to evaluate these areas.

The audit report provides a major source of information about the financial condition of the district and the accounting methods used by the staff. If the audit does not reflect a favorable opinion, board members and the superintendent should be concerned about the fiscal management of the district.

KEY TERMS

Assembly Bill 1200

Audit

Audit committee

Audit procedures

Audit report

Controller

CPA

District annual report

Management report

Net ending balance

No opinion

PA

Qualified opinion

Student Body Fund

Unqualified opinion

DISCUSSION/ESSAY QUESTIONS

1. It is estimated that superintendents spend a minimum of 31% of their time on budget issues. What are the major budget tasks performed by the superintendent? Why is so much time spent on this responsibility?

2. Discuss the legal requirements for an annual audit of school district budgets and the major functions performed by an auditor.

3. The California Controller is charged with fiscal oversight of California school districts. What are the major responsibilities of the controller in this area?

4. Assembly Bill 1200 was approved by the state legislature in 1991. Why was this legislation passed? What are the major components of the bill?

5. After completion of a district audit, the auditor may give any of three opinions regarding a district's fiscal condition. Briefly discuss each of the three opinions and their significance for the district.

CHAPTER 11

STUDENT BODY ORGANIZATIONS

INTRODUCTION

One of the most valuable resources available to a school principal is the school's student government. The student body organization is composed of student leaders elected by their classmates. These leaders offer a valuable source of information and guidance in addressing a wide range of issues that develop within a school community. Student leaders help a principal set the tone for a school and assist in the educational program for all students. Student government participates in such issues as student citizenship, school operations, attendance, student activities, and scheduling and conducting school programs. They help with serious matters like drugs, alcohol, vandalism, and violence within the school community. School morale and pride flourish in a school that strongly emphasizes co-curricular programs along with the academic schedule.

Student body organizations are an integral part of the educational program in most high schools in California. They expand the opportunities available in the regular school setting and provide valuable training for students. Among student organizations are athletic teams, music groups, academic groups, and social groups. Depending upon the size of the school, these groups may number several hundred. A guiding principle for all student body organizations should be maximum student involvement.

Management of and accounting for student body funds are major tasks in many schools, their complexity depending on the size of the school and the extent of its activities. In most schools, the principal has primary responsibility for supervision of student body organizations. In a large high school, he or she may delegate this task to a student activities director, although ultimate responsibility for supervising the program still rests with the principal.

In many schools, particularly secondary schools, the sheer number of student body accounts is a nightmare for the student body clerk and for the principal, who retains ultimate accountability for them. As for school site budgets, discussed above, computer software programs promise to ease the accounting burden. A major source of information for proper accounting of student body funds is a document, available from the California Department of Education, entitled *Accounting Procedures for Student Organizations* (California Department of Education, 1992a). This book is an invaluable tool for accounting personnel and the principal. Guided by this document, districts adopt guidelines for proper accounting for the Student Body Fund. If the guidelines are followed and legal entries made on an ongoing basis, the time spent on this task is minimized.

LEGAL STATUS AND PURPOSE OF STUDENT BODY ORGANIZATIONS

Education Code Section 48930 and the sections following provide the legal framework for the Student Body Fund. Since student organizations are not supported by public funds, they rely on fund-raising to finance their activities. In raising and expending student funds, the student body organization has one basic aim: to promote the general welfare and morale of the students as a whole. Student body funds exist for the sole purpose of supporting non-instructional activities that enhance the overall educational experience of students.

The school district governing board serves as the legal authority for establishment of the fund. The board must adopt regulations that govern student body organizations, supervision of their activities, and financial operations and management. Governing boards must establish procedures for preparation and control of the student body budget. Student body organizations may be allowed to use school properties without charge, subject to regulations set by the school board. These regulations usually delegate day-to-day management of the student body to the school principal.

ESTABLISHMENT OF STUDENT BODY ORGANIZATIONS

When a governing board authorizes establishment of a student body organization, several steps should be taken. A constitution must be written that states the name and purpose of the organization. Minutes should be kept of each meeting and a procedure developed to authorize expenditures. Policies should be developed for approving the student body budget, for fund-raising activities, and for election of officers.

The student body usually acts as an umbrella for several clubs and organizations at a school. Specific procedures should be developed for recognition of school clubs and organizations. A primary requirement is that the group be composed entirely of students enrolled at the school. Student groups must receive approval from the student body organization and the school board or its designee. Often, school boards delegate this responsibility to the school principal.

Each student body organization must develop a realistic budget. The principal or student body advisor trains, guides, and supervises students in this task. A preliminary budget is submitted to the student governing body by May 1 each year. Ordinarily, the budget is reviewed and finalized in October. A budget should include estimated income and expenditures. A reserve should be projected to allow a degree of flexibility in case of unanticipated needs.

STUDENT ACTIVITIES

A majority of funds generated by student body organizations come from fund-raising activities. These activities must promote the general welfare and morale of the entire student body. Some fund-raisers are held at school; others may be outside. Examples of fund-raisers include candy and magazine sales, car washes, dinners, carnivals, and newspaper drives.

Strict federal and state regulations govern sale of food items on campus. Such sales must be authorized by the school board. No food items prepared on the premises by students may be sold during the school day. In elementary schools, food items may be sold after the close of the midday food service period. In high schools, junior highs, and middle schools food items may be sold at any time during the school day, as long as they are not prepared on the premises and the item is not sold by the district food services program on that school day.

Each plan for fund-raising by a student body organization must be approved by the student council and the school principal. The plan must include a recommended method of financial accountability. Fund-raising efforts must be scheduled carefully to avoid conflict with other departments or organizations and should be limited to minimum interference with the school's educational program.

STUDENT BODY ACTIVITY CARDS

Activity cards are commonly sold to high school students. Funds generated by the sale of student body cards can be substantial. In most high schools, the card is priced from $15 to $50. In a school of 2,000 if half of the student body purchases a card, the revenue ranges from $15,000 to $50,000.

These cards typically provide a variety of benefits, including admission to athletic events and school dances, a discount on the yearbook, and copies of the school newspaper. Members of the student council should give careful thought to items furnished to purchasers of a student body card. For example, should the yearbook be included—or purchased separately? The student body organization should set the price of both the student body card and admission to athletic and other school activities. The benefits associated with a student body card should be printed on the card so students know exactly what they are.

ATHLETICS

Fund-raising connected with athletic events must accord with league agreements and conform to policies of the California Interscholastic Federation (CIF). Income may be generated by sale of pre-numbered tickets, the receipt of a guaranteed amount from schools visited, and exercise of radio and television rights. In many schools with a strong athletic tradition, program sales and concessions at the games also generate substantial income.

OTHER FUND-RAISING ACTIVITIES

A variety of other sources may yield profit for student organizations. Publications, vending machines, a student store, school dances, musical events, and donations are utilized by most student body organizations. On the other hand, the California Association of School Business Officials (1988) suggests several activities that should *not* be used to raise funds. These items are listed in Table 5.

STUDENT FEES

The big day has finally arrived. Mom and Dad are so proud of son John, who just graduated from the eighth grade—and with honors, too. The middle school experience is finally over, and John's parents are looking forward to being the parents of a high school student: enrolled in honors math and English, Spanish and biology, band, and athletics. They have never had to worry about John's grades and are very proud that he will be in band and on the freshman football team. Yes, high school should be smooth sailing.

But what is this during freshman orientation? A $100 calculator for math; $125 to rent his saxophone; $75 for gloves, shoes, and socks for band, plus a $20 fee to sign up; a $30 lab fee in biology; $35 for a field trip to the Museum of Tolerance as part of honors English class; and more than $200 for shoes and athletic equipment to play on the freshman football team. The coach said John would need to bring money for meals before and after football games, too.

Table 5

Fundraising Activities <u>Not</u> to Be Used

Activity	Reason Inappropriate
Raffles	Element of gambling
Games of chance	Element of gambling
Animal rides	Safety
Activities involving darts or arrows	Safety
Throwing objects at live targets	Safety
Dunking a person into a water tank	Safety
Destroying old cars or similar objects with hammers, etc.	Safety
Selling used jewelry	Health factors
Rummage sales	Health factors
Trampolines or mini-trampolines	Safety

The shock that John's parents experienced is not unusual in California public schools. Yet these fees are strictly illegal, according to Donald Driftmier (1997), an accountant with Vavrinek, Trine, Day & Company, one of the state's largest auditing firms for California schools. The fees and fund-raisers that keep many programs afloat in public schools conflict with the free education promised in the California Constitution. Driftmier maintains that schools cannot legally charge students to join clubs, band, or athletic programs; or to buy pencils, paper, workbooks, novels, computer disks, calculators, or uniforms. Students may be charged for lunch, or a fee to purchase material for a project the student will take home, such as materials for a wood shop project. However, if the student does not want to take the project home, he need not pay. Students may also be charged for damage or loss of a book or other school property.

Students can voluntarily participate in fund-raisers, but they cannot be excluded from any activity because they do not or will not help raise money. Driftmier said that the law is not followed for two reasons: one is lack of knowledge on the part of teachers and school administrators, and the other is unwillingness to abide by the law. Driftmeier advises the districts he audits that they can meet the legal requirements without losing their programs. Schools need to make sure that they clearly tell parents that the fees or charges are voluntary and explain that they are necessary for the programs to continue. Mentioning that financial assistance is available is not good enough.

In 2000 three parents sued the Pasadena school district demanding a halt to the collection of student activity fees and asked for a refund of money already paid for ID cards, athletic clothes, and notebook organizers. The lawsuit, filed in Los Angeles Superior Court, charged that the practice of collecting fees for extracurricular activities is unconstitutional. The plaintiffs argued that such fees violate the free education clause of the California Constitution and a 1984 state Supreme Court decision that outlawed charges for extracurricular activities. This decision, *Hartzell v. Connell*, established that extracurricular activities such as band and cheerleading are part of the education program and must be provided without fees.

Roger Wolfertz, counsel for the California Department of Education, said the department receives about a dozen parent complaints a year about districts charging mandatory fees. Wolfertz said the department advises districts that the fees are totally illegal, and that such charges should be discontinued.

MANAGING INCOME OF A STUDENT BODY ORGANIZATION

As just indicated, a primary activity of student body organizations is fund-raising. Before monies from the Student Body Fund may be spent, several safeguards must be in place. In particular, all expenditures must receive prior approval, either as part of the approved student body budget or by action recorded in the minutes of a meeting. Moreover, the Student Body Fund should be used to benefit those students who are currently active members of student organizations and have assisted in generating such funds; therefore, large Student Body Fund reserves are discouraged (California Association of School Business Officials, 1988). Gorton (1983) identifies several additional items to be given attention in managing student body organizations:

- school board authorization for the collection of student activity fees

- involvement of students and teachers in establishing and setting the amount of student activity fees and in decisions about how monies are to be spent

- maintenance of school records of monies collected and disbursed, showing that the procedures enumerated below are being followed:

    A receipt is issued to each individual from whom money is received
    A deposit receipt is obtained from the bank to show that all monies have been deposited upon receipt

The amount that is deposited is recorded in a student activities account under the appropriate fund

A requisition form, requiring the signature of the activity sponsor, is used to initiate purchases

Purchases involving large sums of money require the approval of the principal

School checks are used to expend monies and to pay student activities bills

All expenditures are recorded in the student activities ledger where each is listed under an appropriate fund

- monthly preparation of a budget status report for each activity sponsor and for the school administrator

- yearly audit and review of the purposes for which student activity monies have been spent, conducted by the district office with involvement of the school principal and sponsors of activities.

In addition to these guidelines for managing and tracking student organization funds, state regulations prohibit certain expenditures, including:

- equipment, supplies, forms, and postage for curricular or classroom use or for district business

- repair and maintenance of district-owned equipment

- salaries or supplies that are the responsibility of the district

- articles for the personal use of district employees

- gifts, loans, credit, or purchase of accommodations for district employees or other personnel

- contributions to fund-raising drives for charitable organizations (California Department of Education, 1992a).

Because of the volume of student body activities, all monies must be subject to careful collection and verification procedures. Any money collected from any source must be substantiated by pre-numbered student body receipts, pre-numbered auxiliary receipts, pre-numbered class receipt records, cash registers supplying cumulative readings, or other auditable records.

All fund-raising activities must be approved by the principal and the student body organization. Pre-numbered tickets should not be printed in the school printing department. All forms should be controlled by the principal or his or her designee. Whenever tickets are sold, ticket reports and unsold tickets must be available for audit. Whenever possible, money must be collected in the central office. Collections should be deposited in the bank daily—and never left in the school over weekends or holidays.

Accounting procedures for student store sales, sales of food items, fees collected for athletic events, concessions, publications, gifts and grants, yearbook sales, and proceeds from vending machines should be carefully established and monitored. Procedures for the purchase and lease of equipment also should be developed. A number of state and federal regulations, several of which have been noted above, control the sale of food by members of the student body.

CHART OF ACCOUNTS AND FINANCIAL REPORTS

A chart of accounts should be developed by the student body organization to track revenue and disbursements in the various student body groups. Account numbers should correspond to district and state accounting procedures. Accounts include current assets, fixed assets, current liabilities, trust accounts, other liabilities, other accounts, revenues, and expenditures. Trust accounts are generally divided into three main groups: scholarship accounts, class accounts, and club accounts.

Student body officers develop periodic financial reports. A report, or financial statement, lists revenues and expenditures and concludes with a balance sheet. This information compares actual revenue and expenditures with budget projections. In a large high school, financial statements should be prepared on a monthly basis; in a smaller school, with fewer organizations and accounts, a bimonthly statement may be sufficient. Whatever the timeline, these reports enable students, advisors, the principal, and the school board to monitor the financial condition of the organization and to make adjustments where required. Figure 11 provides an example of a Student Body Financial Report.

Figure 11

Sample Student Body Financial Report

**SNOWLINE JOINT UNIFIED SCHOOL DISTRICT
SERRANO HIGH SCHOOL**

Budget Report for October 30, 2000

Account Title	Budget Amount	Actual Amount	Revised Estimate
Basketball	$ 2,250.00	$ 3,038.55	$ 3,039.00
Cap and gown rental	1,200.00	983.73	1,468.00
Coke sales	7,000.00	6,183.75	7,000.00
Drama	550.00	0	550.00
Football	15,000.00	17,235.25	17,236.00
Journalism	700.00	300.50	800.00
Student Store	10,000.00	5,000.25	11,000.00
Wrestling	1,500.00	0	1,500.00
Yearbook	18,000.00	6,250.00	18,000.00
Senior class	6,000.00	2,500.00	6,000.00
Total Expense	62,200.00	41,492.03	66,593.00

AUDITING OF STUDENT BODY ACCOUNTS

A major responsibility of the principal is to ensure that student body accounts are properly maintained. All books, transactions, and records of the Student Body Fund must be open to review and audit. The district is required to perform periodic internal audits and to conduct an annual external audit. Like the audit of all other district funds and accounts, the audit of the Student Body Fund must be performed by an accountant licensed by the State Board of Accountancy who is not otherwise employed by the district.

The California Association of School Business Officials developed the following six guidelines to assist school officials in complying with proper accounting procedures:

- Checks should never be issued to cash
- A complete reconciliation should be kept of cash collected and disbursed; any remaining funds are to be deposited
- Site checkbooks used for field trips should be controlled by the site secretary or a student body controller
- No blank checks should be issued to pay for field trips
- Outside organizations (e.g., booster club, P.T.A.) who sponsor field trips should carry their own insurance, proof of which should be filed at the district office
- All outside organizations are responsible for collecting and depositing funds related to any of their sponsored events
- School personnel are not to sign checks or invoices, do bookkeeping, or serve as an officer of an outside organization (Driftmier, 1997).

The California Education Code requires that district funds pay the cost of the audit. This requirement is intended to ensure strict objectivity by the auditor. The busy principal may find the laws, rules, and regulations related to the Student Body Fund complex and time-consuming. The results are worth the effort, however, because a well-managed program of student organizations pays rich dividends to the principal and staff and safeguards the integrity of the organizations themselves.

SUMMARY

Student body organizations have a very important role in the functioning of a school. They represent an important addition to the educational experiences of students. Regardless of the size of these organizations or the dollar volume of fund-raising activities, the level of accountability must match that required of other funds within the district.

A school district governing board, the superintendent, business manager, and principal have major roles to perform in effective management of a student body organization. Carefully crafted policies, regulations, and guidelines need to be developed to ensure proper accounting for student body funds. A major source to guide the financial aspects of a student body organization is contained in a California Department of Education publication entitled *Accounting Procedures for Student Organizations* (1992a).

It is important to recognize that a major objective of the student body organization is instructional in nature. The decision-making experience involved in developing and managing the student body organization can be invaluable. Students should be provided as much latitude in decision-making as is reasonable, with proper guidance from the principal and staff.

KEY TERMS

Accounting Procedures for Student Organizations

ASB	Pre-numbered tickets
ASB Constitution	Student activities
Charitable organizations	Student body cards
Chart of accounts	Student Body Fund
CIF	Student body reserves
Fund-raising activities	Trust accounts

DISCUSSION/ESSAY QUESTIONS

1. Effective leadership in the Associated Student Body (ASB) can be a great asset to a school's instructional program. Discuss the instructional benefits of the ASB.

2. Discuss the major responsibilities of the principal in supervising the ASB.

3. Student body activity cards may account for a considerable sum of revenues and expenditures in a school. What are the major purposes of the student body card? What accounting safeguards should be established for managing this program?

4. Gorton (1983) discussed several key items in managing student body organizations. What are these key elements?

5. Student body funds are not to be used to supplant the district's obligation to students. What does "supplant" mean? Give examples of expenditures prohibited to the ASB.

6. Procedures for auditing the ASB fund are similar to those for all other district funds. However, this fund is often cited by auditors for improper accounting procedures. What are the most common reasons for this citation by auditors?

CHAPTER 12

TRANSPORTATION

INTRODUCTION

What was once a rural phenomenon has become an accepted, even expected, service in most California communities. Transportation of students to and from school began when the country entered the automotive age. Busing helped make education available to a greater number of children. The busing of students also contributed to the reduction or elimination of the one-room school, as rural students were transported to nearby villages or cities.

In an earlier era it was not uncommon that a teacher, the principal, or some other staff member drove the school bus in addition to his or her primary job. With modern improvements in transportation vehicles and construction of modern roads and freeways, the task of driving a bus has become far more complex and in California, as in most states, is strongly regulated by the state department of education and the highway patrol.

Today, many students ride school buses, rather than public transportation, to reach school. Special education students often need transportation, even for short distances, and often on vehicles equipped to carry equipment such as wheelchairs. In addition to conveying students to and from school, many district transportation systems also carry students to and from a vast array of co-curricular activities, including athletic events and field trips. With increased enrollments and shifting populations come overcrowded classrooms, again leading to transportation to move young people from one school to another. School business officials agree that managing transportation has become a demanding, often frustrating, task and a drain on fiscal resources.

KEY EVENTS

School transportation has come a long way since the horse-drawn wagon. Steve Hirano (2000) developed a summary of the key events that shaped the development of school transportation. With permission of the author, a brief summary of those events follows.

- **1900—Turn of the century.** Eighteen states had laws that approved public funding for pupil transportation.

- **1920—The first school bus chassis.** A 20-seat passenger bus was developed by International Motor Car Company.

- **1926—North Carolina contract for 200 school buses.** Perley A. Thomas Car Works, a streetcar manufacturer, won a contract to manufacture 200 school buses for the state.

- **1939—The first national school transportation conference.** Representatives from the 48 states attended the seven-day conference. The delegates created 44 standards for buses. Among those standards was use of the color yellow as a standard for buses.

- **1954—*Brown v. Board of Education.*** This U.S. Supreme Court decision called for elimination of segregated schools. Its effect on school transportation was to create crosstown busing in many cities.

- **1956—Stopping for school buses.** New York was the first state to approve a law requiring motorists to halt for stopped school buses.

- **1959—First diesel school bus.** The first diesel school bus in the United States was put into operation in North Carolina. Today, it is estimated that 95% of all school buses are diesel-powered.

- **1975—Education of all Handicapped Children Act.** This federal legislation guaranteed a "free and appropriate public education for all children." The legislation greatly expanded the role and cost of school bus operations.

- **1977—Federal Safety Standards.** New federal standards for school bus construction went into effect. The standards dealt with emergency exits, roof strength, seating, fuel system integrity, and hydraulic brake systems.

- **1986—Safety Belts.** New York became the first state to mandate seat belts in all new school buses. The legislation did not mandate use of the belts.

- **1995—Drug and Alcohol Testing.** All districts with 50 or more drivers were required to implement an alcohol and drug testing program for drivers. In 1996, new legislation was approved that required all districts, regardless of size, to implement the testing program.

In many California districts the chief business official supervises the transportation department. As districts become larger, this responsibility may be delegated to a lead bus driver or a transportation supervisor. As the business manager develops a plan for student transportation, consideration should be given to the following policy questions:

- Is the transportation system to be used solely to transport students to and from school?
- If it is used for the athletic and co-curricular program, are there guidelines for mileage, overnight stays, etc.?
- What are state and district walking distances for children of various ages and grades?
- What training programs are in place for bus drivers, mechanics, dispatchers, and supervisors?
- Is it financially and politically wise to contract for student transportation?
- Are routing and scheduling managed in an economical fashion?
- Have long-range plans been made for bus replacement—a major capital outlay expenditure?
- Are accounting methods in place and adequate for proper filing of claims for state reimbursement?

FINANCING SCHOOL TRANSPORTATION

In 1997-1998 some 962,272 California K-12 students rode a bus to and from school at a cost of $1,004,658,122—or $1,044 per pupil. It is interesting to note that in the same year Texas transported more students (1,345,143) at an annual cost of $502 per student. New York state transported almost twice as many students as California (1,729,528) at a yearly cost of $482 per pupil ("School Transportation," 2000).

The major transportation problem confronting school districts is lack of income to meet ongoing costs. Another difficulty is that calculations for reimbursement of transportation costs may result in two districts with the same expenditures receiving different amounts from the state.

Transportation for school districts has been inadequately funded by the state for many years. State funding has not been adjusted for growth in students transported since 1983-84. It has received COLAs in only a few annual budgets since that time and has increased so slowly that scarcely more than half of statewide transportation costs were funded by state aid in 1993-94. The shortfall in transportation has been particularly critical for districts that have experienced an inordinate increase in student enrollment. In consequence of this shortfall, transportation encroachment has become a major drain on most districts' General Fund. Many California districts are spending 5% to 10% of General Fund monies on student transportation.

COMPUTERIZED SCHOOL BUS ROUTING

Computerized school bus routing has enabled many districts to reduce transportation costs. Several software programs have been written for this purpose. An example is a computer system designed by Edulog called Transportation Information Management System (TIMS), which is designed to assist a district in transporting more students with fewer buses. The first step in using TIMS is to digitize maps for the district. Street names, school boundaries, and school locations are designated on a map.

After the map has been completed, student information is entered into the program. If a student is eligible for student transportation, this information is also entered. Students' residences are plotted on the computer screen. These entries may be combined with other demographic data for any area in the district. For example, residences of handicapped students needing special transportation assistance can be tagged.

Next, other details, including minimum distances between stops and the distance a driver may deviate from the general path to the schools, must be entered. Minimum walking distances for the various grade levels are also included. Once all information has been introduced, the computer designs the bus routes.

The computer efficiently creates routes so buses travel only on designated routes and do not backtrack. It also designs the routes so as to observe maximum allowable bus capacity. The computer prints the bus routes, giving directions for the bus driver, names of students assigned to the bus, and locations of stops.

Such a computer program also reviews alternative start and end times for schools to maximize the transportation schedule. Staggering start times can considerably reduce transportation costs. The computer does the number-crunching, calculating all possible configurations and evaluating route times.

AUDITING BUS ROUTES

After all bus routes are established and stabilized for the year, the system must be audited. One way to accomplish this task is to place timers on buses to record the time necessary for pre-trip inspection, cleaning, and actually driving the route. Motion timers are easily installed at a cost of approximately $250 each. The timer records the time the driver starts the route and continues recording until the route is completed. The timer also records any unauthorized stops that occur along the way. The transportation director should monitor all routes for at least two days and record the mileage each day. Time requirements are calculated and additional time added for such duties as warm-up and cleanup. The data collected through this system are useful for payroll and for auditing purposes.

PREVENTIVE MAINTENANCE

The key to a safe, efficient transportation system is well-maintained equipment. Preventive maintenance pays off financially. For example, properly inflated tires increase fuel efficiency, safety, and the life of the tire. Inspection and maintenance are scheduled and tracked for each vehicle. Two additional transportation issues of importance are bus replacement and district charges for home-to-school transportation.

STUDENT SAFETY AND SEAT BELTS

The National Association of State Directors of Pupil Transportation Services has a major goal of ensuring student transportation safety. This organization declares that school buses manufactured after 1977 are the safest form of motor vehicle travel in the United States. There are fewer than ten school bus passenger fatalities each year out of approximately ten billion student trips. In contrast, more than 800 school-aged children are killed in passenger cars during school hours (National Association of State Directors of Pupil Transportation Services, 2000).

Since safety belts were first installed on automobiles, the question has been, "Would seat belts on school buses provide for greater safety?" Several studies have been conducted to answer this question. A major study was completed by the National Highway Traffic Safety Administration (NHTSA) in 2000. The conclusion of the study was that there was no supportable need for lap belts in large school buses.

In 1993, the California Legislature approved Assembly Bill 15, which required that all school buses manufactured on or after January 1, 2002, would have safety belts. The legislation required pelvic and upper torso restraints.

Governor Wilson expressed concern with the research supporting the installation of seat belts but signed the legislation with the requirement that further study should be completed prior to the implementation of the legislation. In 2001, the California Legislature, with Governor Davis's approval, extended the deadline for purchase of the seat belts until 2005.

BUS REPLACEMENT

Bus replacement is woefully underfunded. Prospects of new money for this purpose were bleak for many years. The situation changed in 2000-2001, when $4.2 million were allocated to districts with less than 2,501 ADA for bus replacement and $50 million in one-time funding for all other districts. The California Energy Commission administers the program. The one-time funds must be used to replace pre-1987 diesel-powered buses. Since a new bus costs from $100,000 to $140,000, the available sum will purchase approximately 350 buses. The balance of the appropriation is for the retrofit program required by several air quality management control districts (Goldfinger, 2001).

TRANSPORTATION FEES

In an attempt to offset transportation costs, several California districts began charging student transportation fees. In 1988 the U. S. Second District Court found such fees unconstitutional. However, in April 1991, California's Third District Court of Appeals ruled just the opposite, declaring that home-to-school transportation fees are legal. Since the two cases were in conflict, the California Supreme Court agreed to hear an appeal of the Third Court's decision. In 1992 the California Supreme Court ruled in *Arcadia Unified School District v. State Department of Education* that it is legal for school districts to charge a fee for home-to-school transportation as long as students who cannot afford to pay are exempted from the fee.

The two key issues reviewed in the Arcadia case were these:

- Does the law allowing school districts to charge fees for home-to-school transportation (Education Code 39807.5) violate the free school guarantee in the California Constitution?

- Does the law allowing school districts to charge fees for home-to-school transportation violate the equal protection clause of the California Constitution?

Six of the seven Supreme Court Justices concluded that the answer to both questions was "no." The court's rationale for this decision was that students are not required to use the same means of transportation as their classmates in order to get to school. Individual students may choose different modes of transportation to suit their own circumstances. Unlike textbooks or teachers' salaries, transportation is not an expense peculiar to education. Without doubt, school-provided transportation may enhance or be useful to school activity, but it is not a necessary element that each student must utilize or be denied the opportunity to receive an education, according to the court.

When establishing a fee policy, a district must develop an exemption for parents and guardians who are indigent. Districts may define "indigent" in either of two ways. The same criteria established for the free lunch program may be used, or students whose families are recipients of Aid to Families with Dependent Children (AFDC) may be exempt from transportation fees. In addition, handicapped students eligible for transportation fee exemptions are those whose Individualized Education Plans (IEPs) specify transportation services.

When developing a fee policy, a district must consider two additional requirements of the Education Code. The fees collected in any year may not exceed the statewide average non-subsidized cost of providing transportation on a public transportation system. Neither may they be higher than the district's actual operating cost of home-to-school transportation minus state aid for transportation. In addition, the school board must avoid provisions that carry implications of racial or ethnic segregation.

FEES FOR EXTRACURRICULAR ACTIVITIES

The California Supreme Court decision in *Arcadia* also addressed fees for extracurricular activities. In upholding a fee for home-to-school transportation, the California Supreme Court differentiated a transportation fee from a fee for extracurricular activities. In 1984 the Supreme Court had ruled in *Hartzell v. Connell* that a fee for extracurricular activities violates the free school guarantee embedded in the California Constitution. The court held that the free school guarantee extends to all activities that constitute an integral and fundamental part of elementary and secondary education or that constitute necessary elements of any school's activity. Therefore, the decision in *Arcadia* does not authorize fees for transportation connected to extracurricular activities (Atkinson, Andelson, Loya, Ruud & Romo, 1992).

CONTRACTING FOR SERVICE

With a view to conserving district funds, several California school districts contract with outside firms for student transportation services. The major advantage of contract services for many districts is avoiding capital expenditures for buses. With one bus costing approximately $100,000, vehicle purchases are a major drain on the resources of most districts. Moreover, some districts conclude that contracting for service reduces the annual operational cost of transporting students.

When considering contracting for services, the district should examine the most important variable in student transportation services: transporting students safely and efficiently. Selection of a contractor should start with a thorough understanding of the student transportation needs of the district. That in place, the district is ready to select a contractor who can provide a competitive bid that meets all district requirements, chief among them a safe and effective system.

The goal in writing the transportation contract is to develop a strong working relationship between the contractor and the district. To that end, the contract should be precisely written and reviewed by the district's attorney. Elements to be covered in the contract include management of services, pupil delivery times, training requirements for drivers, safety standards, and vehicle maintenance standards. Procedures for evaluating the services of the contractor are essential. Included in the contract must be a termination clause to be invoked if services are not provided as agreed upon.

SUMMARY

Student transportation is big business in California. With many rural communities that cover hundreds of square miles, student transportation has become a major cost factor in many districts. Overcrowding of schools in urban areas has also resulted in higher transportation costs as young people are moved from one site to another. School boards and superintendents have attempted to offset the skyrocketing costs of student transportation with various strategies, including longer student walking distances, staggered starting and ending times for schools, and fees for student transportation.

Providing safe and efficient student transportation is a formidable problem facing the legislature and taxpayers of this state. Every day thousands of students are transported to and from school in buses that were manufactured before the federal safety standards developed in 1977. Of California school buses, 9% were constructed prior to 1977, the highest percentage in the nation. Only two other states, Washington (8.68%) and Louisiana (69%) utilize more than 5% pre-1977 buses ("Pre-1977," 2000). A major capital investment is required to replace these buses.

KEY TERMS

Arcadia Unified School District v. State Department of Education
Auditing bus routes
Bus replacement
California Energy Commission
Co-curricular activities
Contracting for service

Fee schedule
Preventive maintenance
Transportation fees
Transportation routing
Transportation scheduling
Walking distances

DISCUSSION/ESSAY QUESTIONS

1. Student transportation has an enviable safety record. What are the major factors/safeguards that have contributed to this record?

2. A school board should consider a number of policy questions when planning or reviewing student transportation. Discuss three major issues that should be addressed in board policy.

3. Student transportation can be a major expense for a school district. Discuss three components of an efficient system designed to contain costs.

4. Student transportation fees have become increasingly common in California school districts. What are the pros and cons of charging student transportation fees?

5. The California Supreme Court ruled in 1992 that transportation fees are legal. What was the basis for this decision by the court?

6. Some California districts are considering contracting for student transportation. Discuss the pros and cons of this arrangement.

CHAPTER 13

Maintenance and Operations

Introduction

School facilities are a major investment of citizens of the United States. Most communities take great pride in the appearance of their schools. Often, in fact, a community is judged by its schools. This judgment may be directly related to the academic accomplishments of students, but architectural design, campus cleanliness, and landscaping of school grounds also influence newcomers' judgments of a community's priorities for education.

The physical appearance of the school building is often a home buyer's first evidence of the quality of a district's schools. If schools are judged excellent and inspire community pride, real estate brokers often include this information in their advertising; they also may feature photographs of school sites. Besides offering these advantages in public relations, a well-designed school plant, carefully maintained and neatly kept, directly affects student and staff pride in a campus and exerts a strong influence on student learning.

Definition

Although the words "maintenance" and "operations" are used interchangeably in many school districts, the terms are distinctly different. The maintenance department repairs and replaces buildings and equipment. Repair and replacement of floors, roofs, heating, air conditioning equipment, and broken windows are examples of maintenance. Replanting of lawns, shrubs, trees, and ground cover should be included in the maintenance and operations budget, as should replacement of a sprinkler system. Maintenance keeps the grounds, buildings, and equipment in their original condition through repairs or through replacement with property of equal value and efficiency. If additional value and increased efficiency result from replacements, these additional values should be charged to capital outlay and credited to capital assets.

Operations, on the other hand, include the district's housekeeping routines that keep school plants functional. Operations are regular ongoing tasks that make schools ready for daily use. Operational expenses include utilities and the cleaning of classrooms and facilities. The operations budget also includes gardening, lawn-mowing, moving furniture, setting up a cafeteria, and delivering supplies to classrooms and offices.

Maintenance personnel are essentially repairpersons and may be called simply the "maintenance staff." In larger districts they have specific titles such as electrician, plumber, or carpenter. The operational staff are the housekeepers and cleaners; they commonly have job titles like janitor or custodian.

BOARD AND DISTRICT POLICIES

Every district is advised to adopt board policies regarding its maintenance and operations functions. These policies should include a philosophical statement that provides the community and staff with a vision of board priorities for maintaining and operating schools and should address the following questions:

Shall it be the philosophy of the district to maintain buildings and equipment in the same state of repair as homes and businesses in the district? A commitment in this area empowers the staff to plan a painting schedule, a calendar for re-roofing, and a timetable for replacement of equipment.

What type financial commitment shall the district make to maintenance and operations? This dollar commitment may be calculated as an item-by-item budget for replacement and repair—or as a percentage of the budget with adjustments from year to year for unusual expenses. Unfortunately, in many California districts, as budget cutbacks have become necessary, maintenance and operations allocations have been severely reduced. Ultimately, if buildings and equipment are to return to a high degree of efficiency, taxpayers will face costs accumulated through years of neglect. From a public relations standpoint, it is sometimes difficult to convince taxpayers that a freshly-painted building, a well-manicured lawn, or a smoothly-paved driveway is a good investment.

What shall be the district's philosophy regarding contract maintenance work versus work completed by the district maintenance staff? Work handled by outside contractors means less work, and hence fewer positions, for the district's classified staff. Consequently, contracting out versus in-house work has become a major concern with classified unions and the legislature.

Routine repairs such as minor plumbing and electrical work, repair of minor roof leaks, broken windows, and the like are generally recognized as functions of district maintenance staff. However, depending on the size of the district and the equipment and specializations in the maintenance department, a district may find it advisable and less costly to contract for major repairs. A policy on this subject avoids untold grief and perhaps considerable expense.

What involvement shall the district maintenance staff have in capital improvement projects? The maintenance staff often prefer "building projects." Erecting a new facility is more exciting than routine tasks like oiling the air conditioning equipment or repairing a leaky roof. Nevertheless, a district maintenance staff is employed for just those routine purposes. Capital improvement ventures, on the other hand, typically require large work crews and special equipment. The maintenance staff should not undertake these major projects, thus inevitably neglecting work and increasing repair and replacement costs in the long run.

What shall be the priorities for responding to maintenance requests? The highest priority should be given to items that create a safety problem. Examples include a wiring condition that could give a severe electrical shock to an employee or student, or cracks in asphalt that could result in a playground accident.

Work that is not completed in timely fashion negatively affects classroom instruction and student and staff morale. Therefore, second priority should be given to "necessity for instruction." Examples include repair of dysfunctional equipment in a vocational shop class or a computer lab. The third priority would encompass those items, aesthetic in nature, that enhance the appearance of a campus, but do not relate directly to instruction. Re-seeding a lawn and remodeling an office fall in this category.

What is the board's direction regarding such duties as cleaning of facilities and landscaping? For example, should a classroom be cleaned each day—or every other day? Given the emphasis in California on water and energy conservation, should lawns be maintained only for play spaces, with other areas planted in low-maintenance species? Or should schools preserve beautifully landscaped rose gardens that require considerable care? How shall such an addition to the aesthetic environment of a school be weighed against other budget requirements?

A policy in this area also gives direction to the director of maintenance and a school principal when citizens wish to donate a facility, trees or other plants. It supports administrators in declining donations with little monetary value, but significant implications for maintenance and upkeep.

What is the organization plan for the maintenance and operations department? Board policy should establish an organizational chart that clearly delineates the chain of command and defines specific areas of responsibility for this department. This topic is discussed in greater detail in the next section.

A board that comes to grips with the above topics is better able to engage in long-range planning for facilities. Moreover, it has increased the likelihood of convincing staff and the public of the district's need for funds to maintain facilities.

ORGANIZATION

Organization of maintenance and operations departments varies from district to district. Because the maintenance department has districtwide responsibilities, staff members are usually responsible to a director of maintenance. The director is a line administrator who reports in turn to the district business manager. In smaller districts, however, the director may be directly responsible to the superintendent.

Organizational patterns for operations departments are even more diverse. Some district organizational charts show this employee group directly responsible to a building principal; others, to a director of maintenance. In the former case, the director serves in a staff relationship as an advisor to employees and the principal.

The following principles should be considered when developing an organizational chart for the maintenance and operations department.

- The organizational chart should be approved by the governing board

- Lines of authority should be clearly delineated, showing the direct supervisor for each position or group of positions

- All employees should be responsible only to one direct supervisor, because overlapping of supervisory personnel leads to confusion and misunderstandings

- Job descriptions should be developed for each job classification and should clearly state the supervisor for that classification.

MAINTENANCE AND OPERATIONS BUDGET

Comments appear on the preceding pages about the necessity of an adequate budget for maintenance and upkeep of facilities and equipment. In most districts the budget for this department is exceeded only by certificated personnel costs.

Adherence to the following guidelines assists administrative staff and the board in budgeting properly for this department.

REPLACEMENT AND REPAIR OF EQUIPMENT AND FACILITIES. Each district should develop a master plan for equipment replacement and repair. The master plan should identify critical points for each year and should encompass at least a five-year period. The life span of roofs, plumbing, electrical equipment, boilers, and other major cost items should be plotted and dealt with on a year-by-year basis. The master plan reduces emergency repairs. It avoids large, unplanned expenses that will inevitably occur if an accumulation of roofs, plumbing systems, or other capital outlay items were to need replacement in the same year.

WORK ORDERS. The director of maintenance should establish a work order system to account for repairs efficiently. Most districts use a computer to track and cost out each work order. This information is used to project budget needs for succeeding years.

PERSONNEL COSTS. Procedures for determining personnel costs range from estimating labor on each work order to a yearly determination of the department's budget for salaries and benefits. In most districts tracking labor costs for each job is unnecessary. Nevertheless, the director must ensure that tasks are completed in an efficient and timely fashion. In addition, personnel costs for future years must be accurately projected.

END OF YEAR BALANCE. It is extremely important that the business manager monitor closely the expenditures in maintenance and operations. Many business managers have been embarrassed, and others dismissed from their positions, for failing to do so. An unexpected need to replace a boiler at a cost of more than $40,000 can exceed budget allocations in a hurry.

All personnel costs should be encumbered at the beginning of the year so the business and department managers know how much money will be available after all salaries and benefits have been paid. Close attention should be paid to approval of overtime, substitutes, and extra duty hours. A precise system for controlling these costs is essential.

RESERVE FUND. Since it is virtually impossible to predict the life span of every piece of equipment or the timing of certain repairs, a reserve fund for the unforeseen is a good budget practice. This account should be clearly designated and its purpose communicated to the staff. Some employee groups have accused business managers of "hiding money" by overestimating maintenance and operations budgets, thus tying up funds that could have been available for salaries. Highlighting the need for a maintenance reserve fund and informing staff and citizens of its purpose help to alleviate this concern.

SUMMARY

Attractive, functional, and well-maintained school facilities are often perceived as indicators of an excellent school district. Schools are a source of student, parent, and community pride and deserve to be well maintained. This task is properly the function of the district's maintenance and operations department.

A district that adopts a philosophy and a long-range plan for maintenance and preservation of its campuses clearly establishes a sound organizational design for the department. As a rule, where maintenance and operations funds are prudently provided and monitored, the community perceives its schools as a good investment and education as a high priority.

KEY TERMS

Board policies

Capital improvement projects

Contract maintenance

Direct supervision

End-of-year balance

Energy conservation

Housekeeping

Lines of authority

Maintenance staff

Maintenance

Operations

Replacement of equipment

Reserve Fund

Work orders

DISCUSSION/ESSAY QUESTIONS

1. An argument can be made that a well maintained and attractive school has educational benefits for students. Do you agree or disagree? What priority should be placed on the budget for maintenance and operations?

2. "Maintenance" and "operations" are two words that are often used interchangeably. Discuss the differences between the two terms.

3. Board policies establish priorities for the total educational enterprise. Discuss three topics for inclusion in board policies that would establish a board's priority for maintenance and operations.

4. The budget for maintenance and operations may be a significant percentage of the district's budget. How should the maintenance and operations department be organized for maximum efficiency?

5. School districts have often used a system of "work orders" to keep track of requested maintenance tasks; "work orders" are used to establish maintenance priorities. Discuss three guiding principles that should be used in deciding the importance of a work order.

CHAPTER 14

SCHOOL FOOD SERVICE PROGRAM

INTRODUCTION

Food courts! No lines! Pizzas, chili dogs, and corn fritters! What has happened to the mashed potatoes, "mystery meat," and cold peas world for mass feeding of school children? What has become of "long, gray serving lines"? If school architects, cafeteria designers, and food service personnel have their way, the memory of cavernous dining rooms with long narrow tables and folding chairs will fade away like the daily, dreary food experiences of Charles Dickens' *Oliver Twist* with his plate of gruel served in a decaying English boarding school.

It appears that the typical shopping mall will provide the model for design of food-court arrangements in the future. In secondary schools, it is common to find a variety of food stations, including a salad bar and grill as well as a milkshake counter.

The good news is that many students get their main meal for the day in the school they attend. In California the administration of child nutrition programs is a three-way partnership among the United States Department of Agriculture, the California Department of Education, and the school district. Adherence to federal and state laws requires constant monitoring of food service regulations and guidelines. The bad news is that it takes considerable effort to make the school food service program self-supporting. Nevertheless, strapped boards of education and superintendents are requiring food service programs to carry their part of the budget load.

GOOD NUTRITION AND STUDENT ACHIEVEMENT

Health educators, nutritionists, and physical education experts point to study after study that shows that good nutrition programs result in better classroom achievement and higher academic performance (Saunders, Fee, & Gottlieb, 1999). However, many of the state's public school students receive no nutrition guidelines, eat fast-food lunches served by the cafeteria, and successfully petition to avoid physical education programs. School nutrition experts estimate that one-half of the student population routinely skips breakfast and makes up a quarter of their daily meals from junk food.

A 1997 U. S. Center for Disease Control survey found that more than 70% of high school students were not eating the recommended amount of fruits and vegetables. A federal report, "America's Children: Key National Indicators of Well-Being, 1999," found that only 24% of two- to five-year-olds were following a good diet, and that decreased to only 6% by the time those children were teenagers.

Several national studies have linked nutritious school breakfast programs with academic achievement. In Minnesota and Massachusetts, students who participated in a school breakfast program showed improvement in reading and math scores on tests of basic skills. A Baltimore study showed that skipping breakfast even once a week negatively affected students' problem-solving ability that day (Jeffers, 2000).

HISTORY OF THE FOOD SERVICE PROGRAM

The beginnings of concern for student nutrition can be traced to 1790 in Germany when Count Rumsford organized soup kitchens to feed the hungry children of Germany (Caton, 1990). However, in the United States old schoolhouses were the first sites where meals were prepared for students.

During the depression of 1932 and subsequent war years, the U. S. armed services were forced to turn back many prospective draftees because of malnutrition. Thus, it was seen as in the best interest of the country that children receive at least one balanced meal per day. The National School Lunch Act of 1946 was a consequence of this belief.

NATIONAL SCHOOL LUNCH PROGRAM (NSLP)

The National School Lunch Program was signed into law by Harry Truman and was considered one of the most significant accomplishments of his presidency. The legislation provided assistance to 62,000 schools. The philosophy underlying this program stressed health and nutrition. The overriding concern was taking care of the basic nutritional needs of students so they could focus on their studies, rather than hunger pangs. Another factor behind the legislation was availability of surplus commodities, which are provided to schools by the federal government to supplement commercially purchased food supplies. Thus, the act provided an incentive to school districts in the form of surplus farm supplies and a small cash reimbursement.

This law has remained national policy, with the result that today 95% of all public schools serve to more than 26 million students a daily meal that meets dietary guidelines under the National School Lunch Program ("Federal," 2001).

CALIFORNIA'S FOOD SERVICE PROGRAM

Food service in California schools is big business. This state provides approximately 11% of the school lunches served in the United States (California School Food Service Association, 1994). Approximately one billion dollars in revenue from federal, state, and local income sources are received annually for California's food service program. More than two million children participate in the program every day. Just under one-half of the meals served are free or at a reduced price.

SCHOOL BREAKFAST PROGRAM (SBP)

Another phase of food services, the School Breakfast Program (SBP), was established by an Act of Congress in 1966. Congress recognized that many students were going hungry during the school day, with an adverse educational effect. Therefore, the purpose of the school breakfast legislation was to ensure that students receive a nutritionally balanced breakfast.

In rural communities many students travel long distances to school each day. The breakfast program was originally designed to meet the needs of these children. It was piloted under the Federal Child Nutrition Act of 1966. Subsequently, the program was expanded to all public and nonprofit schools, as well as to residential child care institutions, in the United States.

About 70% of all California schools offer a breakfast program. These schools serve about 16% of the school population, including about 30% of California's low-income children.

Any school may offer a subsidized breakfast program. The federal government reimburses the school district for each meal, and the California Department of Education provides start-up grants up to $10,000 per school to buy equipment, such as coolers for milk (Boyer, 1996).

SCHOOL LUNCH AND BREAKFAST: MEAL CONTENT REQUIREMENTS

Receipt of federal and state reimbursement depends upon meeting nutritional requirements that have been established for school lunches and breakfasts.

LUNCH COMPONENTS. The national school lunch meal pattern was originally developed and implemented in 1980. Government requirements dictate that lunch programs provide approximately 1/3 of the recommended dietary allowances (rda) for good nutrition. The objective is to serve a school lunch that is low in fat, salt, and sugar, but high in fiber. Not every lunch need supply these nutrients; however, the requirements must be met over a period of time.

The following specific nutritional requirements are written into the lunch pattern:

- The carbohydrate requirement may include enriched or whole grain rice, macaroni, noodles, and other pasta.

- The bread requirement is one serving daily and a total of eight servings per week.

- Nuts and seeds may be used to meet 50% of the meat alternate requirement.

- Fruit and vegetable juice may be used to meet 50% of the fruit/vegetable requirement.

- The fruit/vegetable requirement must be met with two or more sources.

- The milk requirement must be met by offering the choice of whole milk or unflavored, low-fat milk. Flavored milk may be offered; however, it is recommended that this decision be made by the local school board and administration.

In 1994 additional dietary guidelines were developed by the U. S. Department of Agriculture. The guidelines require reduction of fat content in school lunches by 30%. No more than 10% can be saturated fat. Schools had until 1999 to comply with the new regulations.

NATIONAL SCHOOL BREAKFAST PROGRAM. The breakfast program emphasizes both iron- and protein-rich foods to enable the student to begin the day. The following requirements for the breakfast program should be met:

- All foods are to be of texture and consistency appropriate to the age group.

- Whole nuts or seeds should not be given to children under the age of five because of the possibility of choking.

- No more than one ounce of nuts and/or seeds may be served.

- Effective July 1, 1989, two servings from one of the following components or one serving from each must be offered: (1) bread/bread alternate, or (2) meat/meat alternate.

- Formulated grain-fruit products may be used as an alternate to meet the bread/cereal and the fruit/juice requirements under the terms and conditions specified by the U. S. Department of Agriculture.

- A juice, fruit, or vegetable that is a good source of vitamin C is recommended to be offered daily.

STATE MEAL PROGRAM

In addition to the federal program, California also reimburses school districts for a part of the cost of food services. Article 11 of the California Education Code provides meal reimbursement funds for participating schools. This code section also mandates that all California public schools serve one nutritionally adequate meal to each child every day. Procedures related to this law are provided in Title V, the California Administrative Code.

SPECIAL MILK PROGRAM (SMP)

California schools that do not participate in other nutrition programs may participate in the special milk program. Students are eligible to receive milk free if they qualify, or to buy milk at a reduced price.

ORGANIZATION OF THE FOOD SERVICE PROGRAM

In most districts, the assistant superintendent of business services or the chief business officer has direct responsibility for the food service department. The business officer usually has a director of food services to maintain control over the program. The director has responsibility for daily operations, purchasing, and budgeting, as well as daily menu planning. Because the state and federal governments supply funds for the program, it is imperative that the director accurately track all income and expenditures. Food service monies are placed in a restricted fund that program directors strive to keep self-supporting.

Some districts operate a kitchen at each school. Others distribute food from one or more central food processing centers to satellites. Still other districts contract with private companies to provide breakfast and lunch.

FEDERAL AND STATE REIMBURSEMENTS

For each meal served on the breakfast program, national school lunch, special milk program, or child care food programs, districts receive a specified amount of reimbursement. This funding is based on whether the meal is offered to students as part of a paid meal, a reduced price meal, or a free meal. The federal government subsidizes all meals with varying degrees of payment, while the state reimburses only those meals consumed by children who are eligible to receive free or reduced meals.

OTHER STATE AND FEDERAL SERVICES TO SCHOOL DISTRICTS

In addition to subsidizing the costs of meals served to students, the national and state governments provide other services. Both the federal and state government offer technical assistance in food storage and preparation, recordkeeping, nutrition education, sanitation, and compliance with federal and state regulations. The U. S. Department of Agriculture donates millions of pounds of foodstuffs for use in school food programs. The department also designates grant money to start district breakfast programs and for menu modification programs.

KEEPING THE SCHOOL FOOD SERVICE PROGRAM SELF-SUPPORTING

One of the major challenges that food service directors face is keeping the food service program on a self-supporting basis. In the past, many districts used the General Fund to help food service programs make it to the end of the year—but no more. The two major expenses in a food service program are personnel and food. In recent years energy costs have also increased expenditures for food services. Food directors must review each of these factors to make a food service program support itself.

PERSONNEL COSTS

Districts have typically paid all personnel costs from the food service restricted fund. However, the General Fund has occasionally "bailed out" this fund by paying for costs such as fringe benefits. But what about support personnel who spend a portion of their time on cafeteria-related duties? A portion of salaries could be paid for the following services: purchasing food, processing invoices, paying invoices, preparing and processing payroll, repairing food service equipment, cleaning the cafeteria, and removing trash and garbage.

One way to avoid overstaffing is to calculate the meals served per labor hour. To complete this calculation, it is necessary to develop a formula to equate à la carte food items with meals. To keep careful track of the food service program, many districts generate a monthly profit-and-loss statement for each school. This statement reports expenses and revenues so schools can track their status from month to month.

SUPPLIES AND EQUIPMENT

The keys to controlling food cost are to hold inventory at its lowest feasible level, to avoid waste, and to restrict use of high-cost food items. Achieving this objective depends upon accurate records and strict adherence to food inventory procedures. Money can usually be saved by combining government commodity food—whether meats, grains, or vegetables—with other ingredients and presenting food items that students enjoy. To control costs, many districts have completely eliminated high-cost food items. For example, one district temporarily eliminated pizza from the menu when cheese was not received as a commodity from the government.

Legitimate Food Service Fund expenditures include new equipment, equipment repair and replacement, and detergent and cleaning supplies. Telephone, postage, and pest control costs may also be charged to the Food Service Fund.

ENERGY COSTS

The district should monitor carefully both gas and electric consumption for meal preparation. With increased rates for electricity, converting an all-electric kitchen to natural gas may be a good investment. The cost of an efficiency audit of air conditioning and refrigeration units may also be money well spent. For example, one high school significantly reduced operating costs by installing a large and a small air-conditioning chiller in place of a single super chiller.

Energy costs may be reduced by structuring the time of meal preparation so expensive energy time periods may be avoided. Otherwise, energy use in school buildings is highest from late morning to early afternoon, rather than at any other time during the day, largely because of immense energy consumption through food preparation.

CONTRACTED OPERATIONS

Even though the majority of school district food programs are governed by a manager employed by the district, a movement among districts to privatize their food service operations is gaining ground. Of approximately 1,000 public school districts in California, 45 chose to privatize their food service operations in 1994-95 (California Department of Education, 1995). This was a 25% increase from the previous year—and an 80% increase over the 1990-91 school year.

Many questions can be raised about contracting with private companies for food service management. Private companies seeking a contract highlight positive attributes of their service. These include increased participation and financial savings. Is there truth to the claims that privatization is more efficient? Why would a school district take a chance on an outside vendor when it already faces strong financial constraints? The possibility of reduced costs is drawing more and more districts to seek private contractors, not only for food services, but also for maintenance, transportation, custodians, curriculum, and data processing systems.

PRIVATE FOOD SERVICE CONSULTING COMPANIES. Food service professionals are called upon to deal with tight budgets, serve quality meals and do so quickly, provide meals to a changing population, and meet all compliance requirements. Some districts believe that fringe benefits and other costs associated with personnel-intensive operations might be better managed by a private company. Such companies as Marriott and ARA have proven themselves in the private sector by producing a quality product.

The chief school business official or superintendent may be under pressure to find new ways to bring costs down. Board members are also under pressure and directly accountable to the public for all aspects of a student's educational program. These pressures set the stage for the board and superintendent to give a private company opportunity to take over the food service program and save the district money.

Why are school food service programs attractive to private companies? The answer is that a classified staff is already in place, and usually a central kitchen stands ready for operation. Most food service procedures are ready to be taken over by a company. The cost of making improvements in the food service operation is borne by the cost per meal.

Private companies have encountered mixed success in this venture. Therefore, it is difficult to evaluate the success of a private company. How might this be measured? First, one might note how many years the company has been in business. Does the private company have a success record in other districts? Lacking better measures, one usually turns to the "bottom line" as the best indicator.

FOOD SERVICE MANAGEMENT COMPANIES AND FOOD SERVICE FUND BALANCES. McCann (1995) studied the ending balances of school districts that had and had not contracted for private food services. She studied the fiscal operations of 47 school districts in each category from 1990-91 to 1993-94. She found that California public school districts that retained the services of private food management services were not guaranteed better financial status in the cafeteria fund balances. In fact, a greater number of districts that operated their own program did better on the ending balance.

DONATED COMMODITIES

The commodities program supplies food to schools in two ways. The first, which makes up a majority of the food served, is called "entitlement commodities." Schools choose these commodities, and the U. S. Department of Agriculture purchases them to send to the schools. These commodities include flour, oil, ground beef, chicken, turkey, canned peaches and pears, and tuna.

The second category is "bonus" or "surplus commodities." These are purchased by the U. S. government when farmers produce so much of a product that sales on the open market would not yield enough to keep them in business. The government buys the surplus to keep prices steady. Most farm products are the same products, such as milk and cheese, that schools use continuously in their food service program.

For the past few years there has been a reduction in federally donated commodities, forcing an increase in district expenditures for food. This increase has, in turn, reduced the ability of many districts, even those with high free and reduced-price meal eligibility, to operate a completely self-supporting program. Another factor that may influence the commodities program is trade agreements that the U. S. may sign, e.g., the North American Free Trade Agreement and the General Agreement on Tariffs and Trade. These agreements may offset the availability of commodities and affect their cost.

INCREASED REVENUES

To increase food sales, the food service director, principal, and staff must focus on the client, the student. Competition for students' dollars by off-campus restaurants, student body sales, and other fund-raising activities forces administrators to active marketing of school nutrition programs. Quality customer service is the best way to market the food service program. Like any business, school food service must be customer-oriented to succeed.

Successful programs involve students in selecting menus and recipes. Food courts and an à la carte line for quick service have greatly increased student participation in the school lunch program. At secondary schools salads, pizza, baked potatoes, hamburgers, tacos, and soup have become common staples.

Members of the Associated Student Body can play key roles in promoting the food service program. Students are influenced by their peers, particularly at the secondary school level; thus, if student leaders are supportive of the food service program, a major step will have been taken toward encouraging students to eat lunch in the cafeteria. The successful food service director spends time with teenagers, observing the latest trends and interests, to design a program that responds to their preferences.

To encourage elementary students to eat school lunches, the food service director must first get students interested in the cafeteria. The principal and food service director can create this interest by inventive menu descriptions, contests, and occasionally inviting parents to join the students at lunch in the cafeteria.

Attention must also be directed to promoting participation by members of the school staff. For instance, many schools have designed attractive dining areas for the staff. Teachers should also be given opportunity to request menus and to suggest strategies to encourage students to eat lunch on campus.

TRENDS IN FOOD SERVICES

District food service programs are big business. As such, they experience many of the same ups and downs as other businesses. Reductions in funds and commodity donations from state and federal governments have forced food service programs to consider several changes. Since students can easily access commercial fast foods, school food programs have begun to offer more à la carte selections and in greater variety. To this end, food carts and specialty centers are on the increase; they extend advertising for the food service program beyond the cafeteria. Many schools attract students to the cafeteria by playing music in the serving area. Others keep students on campus by holding pep rallies and other school events during the lunch period.

Some schools have turned to fast food and soda companies, like Del Taco and Burger King, for part of the daily meals. Cafeteria managers have found that children will eat at school more often if fast food is available. Although these meals may not be the most nutritious, they increase the likelihood that children are eating at least something.

Many California schools are trying to make certain that children are not only eating, but eating well. The Berkeley Unified School District received national attention by serving organic foods in its breakfast and lunch programs. The Corona-Norco District has gained a reputation for a highly successful food service program by decorating each cafeteria with a theme—baseball, popular movies, music, and other themes that young people find comfortable and inviting.

SUMMARY

Given more than 50 education codes affecting school food service programs, the program requires major attention from school district managers. School food service directors are continually forced to ensure that their feeding programs are self-supporting and not a drain on the General Fund. It is obvious that along with this demand, other trends will emerge:

- Greater attention will be given to the student client to encourage nutritional education and eating habits.

- The installation of the food court will become a common practice, particularly in secondary schools.

- The development of the fast food trend will continue.

- Additional districts will contract out for food service operations.

KEY TERMS

Burger King
Central kitchen
Child Nutrition Act of 1966
Contracted services
Donated commodities
Energy costs
Lunch components
Marriott Corporation
NSLP

Nutrition requirements
Personnel costs
Reimbursements
School Breakfast Program
School Lunch Act of 1946
Serving lines
Special Milk Program
State Meal Program
U. S. Department of Agriculture

DISCUSSION/ESSAY QUESTIONS

1. Discuss recent trends in school food service programs. What are the benefits and drawbacks of these trends?

2. Child nutrition programs are jointly sponsored by federal, state, and local government. What is the role of each level of government in the child nutrition program?

3. The school food service program is designed to ensure that students receive a well-balanced meal. What are the nutritional requirements of the school lunch program?

4. Most school districts attempt to operate the food service program so that it is financially self-supporting. Discuss three important factors that must be considered to achieve this objective.

5. Do you believe a school district should or should not have a food service program? Justify your answer with appropriate sources and data.

CHAPTER 15

FACILITIES: A CALIFORNIA CHALLENGE

INTRODUCTION

With the end of the cold war, public education replaced national defense as the number one political issue. How to fix public schools was debated at the local, state, and national levels during the 1990s and early 2000s. It was a major campaign issue in the presidential contest between Bush and Gore in 2000.

The primary focus of the education debate has centered primarily on student learning, but a secondary issue is the need for additional classrooms and the maintenance and upgrading of school facilities. The National Center for Educational Statistics (2000) estimated that K-12 public school enrollment would increase by one million students between 1999 and 2006 to reach a total of 44.4 million students. Nationally, the average age of public school buildings to house those students is already 42 years, and 73% are 30 years old or more.

Meanwhile, pressure is building to support facilities needs. In 2000 the American Civil Liberties Union (ACLU) filed a lawsuit charging California with responsibility for substandard conditions in its urban schools. The ACLU bases its suit on a five-month study of education in California. The study included interviews with parents, students, and teachers. Among the many charges filed in the suit, the most pertinent regarding school facilities include:

- There are no specific standards requiring public schools to provide heat in winter

- There are no clear state requirements that schools have functioning toilets

- There is no regulation to protect students from infestations by rats and cockroaches ("ACLU," 2000).

The National Education Association ("Modernizing," 2000) completed a study of school facilities and found that more than 20 million students attend schools that are ill-equipped for classroom computers. States need $322 billion for school construction, approximately 10 times what they are currently spending. The federal General Accounting Office estimated that the nation's schools needed $112 billion for repair and update of buildings. New York tops the list with a need for $51 billion in construction funds, with California in second place at $33 billion. Most of the school construction cost estimates cover bricks and mortar, but $54 billion are needed to wire schools for computer technology.

FACILITIES IN CALIFORNIA

In California, recent demographic studies indicate that the next generation of students will arrive at the schoolhouse door in larger numbers and in greater diversity than ever. Estimates of anticipated growth in the K-12 student population over the next several years range from 100,000 to 200,000 additional students annually.

California's K-12 student enrollment is equal to the combined populations of Wyoming, Vermont, Alaska, North and South Dakota, Delaware, Montana, and the District of Columbia. The California Department of Education (2000a) placed K-12 school enrollment at 6,050,895 in 2000-2001. The department projects an enrollment of 6,131,614 in 2001-2002, growing to seven million by the year 2008.

A large percentage of the growth is due to immigration, and there is no indication that it will slow down. Approximately 25% of the nation's immigrants are settling in California, predominantly in the San Francisco and Los Angeles areas. Historically, population growth has clustered around the state's major metropolitan areas. However, this trend has changed in California during the past decade. Rapidly escalating land and housing prices are forcing many home buyers to settle in outlying, lower-cost housing markets located up to two hours' drive from the population centers in which they work. This phenomenon has been particularly evident in San Bernardino, Riverside, and San Diego counties. The resultant increase in student enrollment has heavily impacted smaller districts adjacent to large metropolitan areas. These districts rarely have the capacity within existing funding sources to finance construction of facilities needed to house the increased enrollment. Yet, if the state is to avoid undue overcrowding, this growth translates to seven new classrooms every 24 hours. In total, according to a 1998 report, California was at that time already in need of an additional 456 schools to house new as well as current students (EdSource, 1998a).

HISTORY

Lack of facilities is not a new problem. California has experienced steady growth in student population with consequent need for new schools ever since it became a state in 1850. Finance for school facilities has passed through three distinct phases. Phase one began with adoption of the California Constitution and ended in the years following World War II. During this phase the cost of school construction was borne by the taxpayers in local school districts. The key to success was local voter approval to issue General Obligation Bonds (GO Bonds) in an amount up to 5% of assessed property valuation (10% in unified districts). More than half of all present facilities were built during that time.

During phase two, from the end of World War II to the passage of Proposition 13 in 1978, GO Bonds were still the primary vehicle for funding school construction. However, many school districts were swamped with growth in student enrollment during that period and reached the limit of their bonding capacity. Consequently, the state entered the school construction arena in the late 1940s, on an emergency basis, and granted help to some of the most impacted districts. This stopgap effort led to adoption in 1952 of a state school building program under which the state legislature implemented construction aid to school districts that continued for 26 years, until 1978.

Under this plan the first responsibility was placed on the local school district, which had to bond itself to capacity. Once bonding capacity was reached, the state advanced enough funds to house the projected student population. These funds were loaned to districts, to be paid back to the state by formula over 30 to 40 years. By this method, the state used its credit to extend the credit of the local district. The formula included an equalization factor in that low-wealth districts were the first to participate in the state program. Districts with greater resources were expected to continue to fund school construction without state aid. This program worked well until 1978.

Phase three started after the passage of Proposition 13 in 1978. Since Proposition 13, property taxes have been limited to 1% of assessed valuation. General Obligation (GO) bonds, with redemption supported by a local *ad valorem* tax, were no longer possible. This limitation has reduced school districts' ability to raise funds for any purpose, including facilities construction. Therefore, to continue to build schools, the state assumed a major role in construction financing.

School districts continued unable to use GO Bonds for school construction for an eight-year period, from 1978 to 1986. Then, in 1986, Proposition 46 was approved by California voters, restoring to school districts the authority to seek voter approval for bond issues. Nevertheless, the state continued as the major source of funds for school construction. This circumstance stemmed largely from the state's ability to pass a bond issue by simple majority, whereas districts were required to obtain approval of 2/3 of voters. In the year 2000, however, a voter initiative reduced the 2/3 requirement to 55%.

The primary effect of the changes in financing of school construction, as in school finance generally since 1978, has been a shift of local control to the state. The state exerts extraordinary control in determining when and where school facilities are built. It remains to be seen whether the change from a 67% to a 55% majority will return any of this power to school districts.

FINANCE AND FACILITIES

The state's capital investment in school buildings is already massive. California has approximately 8,000 public schools composed of 55,000 buildings that cover approximately 450 million square feet. These structures have a replacement value of $60 billion. Of these buildings, 55% were constructed prior to 1965, and 60% are already overcrowded. The U. S. government's General Accounting Office concluded that California has the worst school infrastructure in the nation, with 87% of its public schools suffering from poor lighting, heating, acoustics, or air quality (Legislative Update, 1996). The Legislative Analyst's office estimates that one in three California K-12 students attends a school that is overcrowded or in need of significant modernization (Legislative Analyst's Office, 2001).

At the present time the major means of financing school construction dollars is a bond issue approved by voters. Typically, the state makes principal and interest payments on bonds over a period of 20 years. Revenues for these payments come from state income taxes, sales taxes, and corporate profit taxes.

Bond measures have been placed on the state ballot for the June or November election in even-numbered years. Occasionally, such a measure has been placed on both the spring and fall ballots, as was the case in 1992. Since passage of a bond measure is not guaranteed, funding is precarious at best. California voters passed a large $1.9 billion bond issue in June 1992, and an additional $900 million issue in November 1992. The next successful bond measure was approved for $2 billion in March 1996. Two years later, in November 1998, Proposition 1A, a $9.2 billion bond measure, was approved by California voters. Money authorized by these statewide bond elections has been depleted almost immediately upon approval, due to the backlog of applications in line for funding.

At the same time, the governor, state treasurer, legislative leaders, and some members of the financial community are concerned with the increasing bonded indebtedness in the state, since bond obligations must be paid each year from the state's General Fund. The Legislative Analyst's office says debt service will soon top $2 billion a year, becoming one of the largest single outlays in the budget. The growing use of state bonds to support the state's infrastructure needs—prisons, roads, hospitals, and K-12 and higher education facilities—has surpassed the 5.4% of general fund spending considered by bond authorities to be the prudent limit. Educators are concerned that California's emphasis on the need for new prisons will drain away much-needed funds for school construction.

In the face of burgeoning demands for remodeling and construction, local school boards, state officials, and the educational community have created a variety of strategies to finance school construction. The major strategies are discussed in the following paragraphs.

SCHOOL BUILDING LEASE/PURCHASE PROGRAMS— LEROY GREENE FUNDS

The Leroy Greene Lease/Purchase program makes funds available for school construction when funding eligibility is met. Eligibility is based on state-developed criteria that define inadequate student housing. The square footage allocation to districts is based on a policy established in the early 1950s and differs according to level—elementary, middle/junior high, or high school. Under this formula an average California classroom covers 960 square feet, among the smallest in the nation.

Leroy Greene funds may also purchase school sites. This allocation also differs by school grade levels. Generally, the state allocates a maximum of 10 acres for an elementary school, 20 acres for a middle or junior high school, and 40 acres for a high school site. Most educators agree that both the square footage and the acreage allocation are inadequate to the educational needs of students in the 21st century.

School districts are allocated monies according to a point system. As of January 1, 1987, districts must match from local monies the funds they receive from the state. In addition, 30% of district classrooms must be relocatable. Priority is given also to districts that have at least 30% of elementary students on a multi-track, year-round program.

Application for state funds is complicated and time-consuming. Much technical knowledge and skill are required to obtain Leroy Greene funds. Because the first three to five years are consumed in moving an application through the system, the program has a reputation as a bureaucratic process that is exhaustive and layered with paperwork. The lease/purchase timeline takes five to seven years from the time a need is identified to completion of construction.

Distribution of Leroy Greene monies for school construction is determined by the State Allocation Board (SAB). This seven-member group is composed of four members of the California legislature and one representative each from the Department of Finance, the

Department of Education, and the Department of General Services. The SAB also leases relocatable classrooms to school districts and uses income from those leases to purchase more portable units.

Since funds are not available to meet the needs of every district within the state, districts are forced to compete with one another for available dollars. Districts applying for funds must justify their request, with the result that districts that are most skillful and energetic in their presentations often receive the funding. Many districts have employed lobbyists and school facility specialists in hopes of obtaining the maximum possible funds from the State Allocation Board. This factor places at a disadvantage those small districts with personnel and resources too limited for the employment of lobbyists or consultants. Districts represented by powerful legislators who lobby for construction funds for the district also hold an advantage over districts without such influence. Finally, district administrators find it very frustrating to work through the process, meeting all eligibility requirements, only to discover that no money is available.

The state school facilities program also includes the Deferred Maintenance Fund, Asbestos Abatement Fund, and Incentive Program for Year-Round Schools. In the early 1980s tideland oil revenues supported the Leroy Greene program. However, the primary source of funds has become the sale of state General Obligation Bonds approved by voters, as discussed above.

LOCAL FUNDING OPTIONS

DEVELOPER FEES. Developer fees levied on new residential and commercial construction provide another option to fund school construction. The School Financing Plan of 1986 authorized school districts to levy school facility fees on residential and commercial developers when new housing construction creates a need for new school facilities. Prior to 1986, developer fees for school construction varied widely throughout the state. Some school districts had no means of financing needed facilities, while others levied charges in excess of $10,000 per new home.

The 1986 law limited school construction fees on new residential development to $1.50 per square foot and fees on commercial/industrial development to 25¢ per square foot. An inflation factor, provided for in the law, allowed the fee to increase in 2000 to $2.05 for residential and 33¢ for commercial/industrial development.

Developer fees were originally conceived as a vehicle to provide interim housing for students. Therefore, the income from such fees is not sufficient for the complete cost of a permanent facility. Duffy (1990) estimates they may provide 40% to 50% of the cost of land

and construction. One estimate indicates that developer fees of $5.17 per square foot would generate sufficient revenues to construct schools (Bowie, 1992).

The mechanism by which developer fees are imposed depends upon a district showing that new housing creates a need for new schools. Having done so, the district has authority to establish developer fees as a condition of the issuance of building permits by the responsible government agency. Cities and counties may impose three types of fees on developers: impact fees (SB 201), city or county fees, and mitigation fees. Impact fees may be spent on interim facilities for a five-year period. Mitigation fees reduce the impact of housing developments on existing school facilities.

Developer fees are an important source of funds and should be collected by districts that are able to justify them. The current developer fee program allows districts the option of using the income as a local match to a state-funded project, a 50/50 or fast-track state-funded project, or—in districts that do not participate in the state Lease/Purchase Program—a wholly district-funded project. Using developer fees within the district has the advantage of circumventing the time-consuming state process. A serious disadvantage, however, is that developer fee income is typically inadequate to build new schools.

DEVELOPER-DONATED SCHOOLS. A developer may legally donate a school to the district in lieu of paying developer fees. Should this occur, the advantage to the district is that all other fees may be eliminated. Unfortunately, this action is rarely taken by a developer.

CERTIFICATES OF PARTICIPATION (COPs). School districts that can handle long-term debt have the option of issuing certificates of participation. COPs are similar to bonds in that they secure funding for capital projects by means of a promise to pay principal and interest to the investor over a period of time. They are not secured by a tax increase, as are general obligation bonds. These negotiable certificates are issued by a district indirectly, through a specially created nonprofit corporation and trustee. Certificates of participation are sold by an underwriter to investors. Because they are secured by the financial integrity of the school district rather than an increase in taxes, voter approval is not required, and income may be used to purchase either real or "personal" (equipment, etc.) property.

The COP debt must be serviced by the General Fund. When COPs are issued to finance new construction, the nonprofit corporation leases the building to the district, the district pays rent from its General Fund, and the investors have an undivided percentage interest in those lease payments. It is common for school districts to service their COP debt from developer fees. Districts may also sell or lease surplus property and apply that income to the annual COP obligation. Proceeds from a pass-through of Redevelopment Agency funds may be also be used to pay the debt.

The payments on COPs are a primary demand on the revenues of school districts that elect this method of school funding. Thus, COPs are viable only for districts that foresee sufficient income to retire the debt. Many districts lack the resources necessary to back certificates in the amount needed to build schools.

LOTTERY FUNDS. Lottery funds may be used to purchase personal property and some real property and for remodeling. The same amendment to the state constitution that established the lottery also forbids expenditure of these funds for construction of new facilities. There is much confusion and misunderstanding among members of the general public about the amount of funds generated by the lottery—not even close to the amount needed for facilities construction—and about the ways in which those funds may be used.

LOCAL GENERAL OBLIGATION (GO) BONDS. Although local bond elections were eliminated by Proposition 13, they were reinstated in 1986 by passage of Proposition 46. This proposition was an important restoration of capital outlay funding ability to school districts. School districts could form special districts to sell construction bonds, subject to approval by 2/3 of the voters in the special district. Meanwhile, funds to repair or replace structurally unsafe buildings required approval by a simple majority of district voters.

Between 1986 (when authority of school districts to place GO Bonds on the ballot was restored) and 1999, some 450 bond issues were placed on a ballot. Of these, 243 received the required 2/3 approval, a rate of 54%. Had the vote requirement been a simple majority during this time, the success rate would have been a spectacular 94% ("Voters," 1999). Consequently, the educational community attempted several times to change the requirement for passage of a GO Bond measure from 2/3 to a simple majority vote. California citizens considered measures to make the change to a simple majority requirement in 1993 and again in the spring of 2000. Both attempts failed. As a compromise, the educational community agreed to place Proposition 39 on the fall 2000 ballot. This proposition, lowering the required vote from 2/3 to 55%, was approved by voters.

Voter approval allows a school or special district to sell bonds to be retired by imposing an *ad valorem* tax on the property tax rolls of the district. Bonds issued by the district represent a promise to pay principal and interest to the investors over a period of time limited to a maximum of 25 years. The bonds are popular with many investors, as the interest earned is tax- exempt at both state and federal levels.

Proceeds from the sale of bonds may be spent only to acquire or improve real property (land or buildings, structures, or fixtures and fences erected on or affixed to the land). The funds cannot be used to purchase furniture, equipment, or services necessary to open a new school.

Placing a bond issue on the ballot is not very complicated. The school board decides how much money is needed to construct schools and votes to place the measure on the local ballot. While the process is not very difficult, convincing voters to approve such a measure is a complex matter in most districts. If local resistance is strong, passing a bond initiative is next to impossible.

MELLO-ROOS COMMUNITY FACILITIES DISTRICT (CFD). In 1982 the state government approved an additional means of financing schools through the Mello-Roos Community Facilities Act. This act gave local districts authority to establish a Mello-Roos district, enabling them to raise revenue to build and maintain schools, libraries, and roads without a general tax increase. Establishing a Mello-Roos district on vacant land is possible and preferred by some developers. Residents of a Mello-Roos district are charged a fee based on their home's assessed value and the amount of funds to be raised.

A school district may go to its community to request funding of a CFD. Such a district may be formed districtwide or in a portion of the district. An advantage in some school districts is that the boundaries of the Mello-Roos district need not be contiguous with those of the school district. The necessary bonding capacity and tax rate are placed before the voters and require 2/3 approval among residents who are affected by the plan.

A second method of forming a Mello-Roos Community Facilities district is to encompass vacant development land and enact a tax on development as it occurs. This method also requires the same 2/3 yes vote, but on the basis of one vote per acre of land. Where there are 12 or less property owners, as may be the case with a development under construction, a mailed ballot is allowed. A developer may prepay varying levels of the tax, thereby controlling the amount of tax to be paid by homeowners. As the homes are built and occupied, the tax activates and provides the necessary funding for school facilities. Because the tax formula is flexible and taxes need not go into effect until homes are built or occupied, developers often prefer this method for funding school construction. The cost is passed on to future home buyers in the form of annual property taxes.

On a recent successful CFD election, the district exempted properties owned by senior citizens and set different rates for homeowners of newly-constructed or newly-purchased homes. An advantage of a Mello-Roos district is elimination of Office of Local Assistance involvement, but like any approach to voters asking for higher taxes, this option requires careful planning and preparation on the part of school district and legal staff.

PARCEL TAX. School districts may hold parcel tax elections to acquire funds to finance the construction of schools. A parcel tax may be variable, like a Mello-Roos assessment, or it may be a flat per-parcel amount. It may not, however, be levied in direct proportion to assessed valuation. This strategy features ease of implementation, but may be difficult to justify legally. The disadvantages are that the election must be held across the entire district and that 2/3 of the electorate must vote for approval before a parcel tax can be enacted.

SALES TAX. A change in state sales tax requires legislative action and the governor's approval, with no election required. Nevertheless, considering the California political climate, an increase in state sales tax is not readily obtainable. However, approval by 2/3 of the electorate may also institute a local sales tax.

RELOCATABLE SCHOOLS. The great majority of California districts use some portable classrooms, but no one knows exactly how many; no state agency maintains an official statewide count. In 1998 the California Auditor General estimated that 72% of all California school sites had portables and that these classrooms housed approximately 27% of the state's public school enrollment (EdSource, 1998a).

With development money so difficult to obtain and creative options limited, many districts are stretching their capital improvement dollars by purchasing relocatable classrooms. An entire school may consist of relocatable buildings: classrooms, offices, bathrooms, work areas, and cafeteria. These schools have a particular advantage in that they can be constructed in a short period of time. In some districts they have been referred to as "instant schools." While this term is not quite accurate, it is true that the timeline is considerably shortened. For one thing, relocatable classroom designs are already approved by the Office of State Architecture. Neither must an application be submitted to the State Allocation Board, a time-consuming process. The interval necessary to construct a relocatable school is certainly much shorter than the two- to seven-year period to obtain funding for and construct a permanent school.

Relocatable schools cost less than permanent structures in that the price of purchasing and preparing the site for a relocatable classroom is about $35,000 to $100,000, as compared with $115,000 to $177,000 for a permanent classroom (EdSource, 1998a). On the other hand, a major disadvantage of the relocatable classroom is an increased cost of heat and air-conditioning. In most cases, each unit has its own thermostat and is subject to the environmental preferences of the teacher in that classroom.

Relocatable classrooms no longer fit the 12' by 60' cramped image that characterized the trailers that have been located on many school campuses. The modern relocatable is very similar to a permanent classroom, having one or more windows, board space, and storage facilities for instructional supplies and equipment. In addition to the advantages of speedy construction and lower cost as compared to permanent buildings, a relocatable is just what the name implies—able to be moved to another location. Thus, as a district's student population shifts, the relocatables can be moved from one part of the district to another. Some districts start each new school with relocatables while permanent construction is taking place on the same site. Then, when the permanent school is finished, the relocatables are moved to another site, where the process begins all over again.

SALE OF SURPLUS PROPERTY. Districts that own surplus school sites or other surplus property may turn that real estate into an asset to provide one-time or long-term income for facility needs. State law provides that a district may sell surplus property, but the district must use the proceeds from that sale for capital purposes, if it has capital needs. Alternatively, districts may lease property and may joint-venture with private entities to receive income or facilities in place of income.

The sale of property should be carefully reviewed by an attorney experienced in this field of law and by a competent financial advisor because certain procedures within statute may contribute to problems in converting surplus property assets into income. For example, Education Code Section 39390 may require school districts to sell surplus school property to cities at a price far below market value.

Another resource may be a valuable site that can be traded for less expensive property plus enough funds to construct a new school. For example, two Southern California districts traded or sold property that was used by the investor to construct a shopping mall and industrial complex. With proceeds from the sale of this commercial property, the districts purchased other sites and constructed new schools. Unfortunately, this is a rare circumstance, as few districts have surplus property of that value. To summarize this section, ten funding alternatives for school construction and voter requirements for each are presented in Table 6.

Table 6

**Nine Funding Alternatives for School Construction
and Voter Requirements**

Program	Requires Voter Approval
State Lease/Purchase	No
General Obligation Bonds	Yes -55% vote
Mello-Roos (CFD)	Yes - 2/3 vote
Parcel Tax	Yes - 2/3 vote
Sales Tax (local)	Yes - 2/3 vote
Sales Tax (state)	No
Developer Fee	No
Developer-Donated Schools	No
Certificates of Participation	No

COURT DECISIONS

In 1986 the Mira Development Corporation requested the City of San Diego to make a land zone change from single-family to multi-family residential. Citizens opposed this request, arguing that the change would increase traffic, overburden limited park facilities, and send more children to an overcrowded school district.

The Sweetwater High School District had requested the City of San Diego to declare a building moratorium in May 1986. In 1987 the district formally opposed the re-zoning because it could not house the additional students anticipated from the higher-density project. The county denied the re-zoning because of its negative impact on traffic, parks, and schools, after which the Mira Development Corporation sued. The corporation cited Government Code Section 65996, which prohibits cities and counties from aiding overcrowded schools.

Fortunately for schools, the court did not agree. This decision, in the case *Mira Development Corporation v. City of San Diego* ("*Mira* decision"), found that cities and counties could deny re-zoning if approval would have a negative impact on schools. The court did not require cities and counties to consider schools when making a legislative decision. However, it did provide them with the authority to do so if they desired. The city of San Diego had in its General Plan an objective that ensured that public services would keep pace with developments. The *Mira* Court found this provision to be significant in reaching the conclusion that the city acted within its discretion in considering the adequacy of school facilities when it denied the re-zoning application.

Many educators and citizens thought that the *Mira* decision would be overturned by a higher court. However, in 1991 the decision in the *William S. Hart Union High School District v. Regional Planning Commission of the County of Los Angeles* case ("*Hart* decision") confirmed the *Mira* decision by stating that cities and counties could include in their General Plans the impact on schools of new construction developments.

The *Hart* decision was followed by a suit in Riverside County. This decision, rendered in 1991 in *Murrieta Valley Unified School District v. County of Riverside* ("*Murrieta Valley* decision"), upheld the *Mira* and *Hart* decisions and stated that the court had a responsibility to consider the impact of legislative decisions on schools. This case gives counties the authority to stop or slow development by reducing residential density or imposing controlled phasing of residential development to mitigate adverse impact on schools.

The California Supreme Court was asked to hear all three cases and declined. This action allows the lower court decisions to stand. School districts can thus rely on these decisions when working with cities, counties, and developers to ensure that schools are built as a result of new construction that will impact schools. However, the effects of the court's decision were short-lived due to passage of Proposition 1A, the $9.2 billion bond measure, in 1998. A clause in this proposition suspended the court's decision for a period of eight years. This clause means that developers, not cities and counties, regained the right to decide land use as it applies to schools. The ability of government agencies to deny school projects will be restored only if a statewide bond measure fails after 2006.

COALITION FOR ADEQUATE SCHOOL HOUSING (CASH)

Proposition 13 prompted a group of superintendents, facility planners, architects, developers, financial institutions, attorneys, and consultants to form an organization to lobby for state funds to build schools. This organization is called the Coalition for Adequate School Housing (CASH). CASH is a statewide lobbying organization with more than 650 members. Its purpose is to develop and support new statewide bond and funding alternatives for school construction. This coalition developed an eleven-point program designed to achieve its objectives:

1. School districts should have authority to pass local funding measures by majority vote.

2. The state should continue capital outlay funding at the current level to supplement local efforts.

3. Legislation should ensure that school facility needs are included in the assessment of community infrastructure needs.

4. The state should maintain an ample school construction fund.

5. Local funding should be maintained at a minimum level before state funds are made available.

6. The state should assume a constitutional obligation to provide minimal facilities to those districts that are unable to raise the required minimum level of local funding.

7. Building construction should be of high quality so that deferred maintenance is gradually phased out.

8. A rehabilitation program should replace the existing modernization program to update older facilities to meet Education and Building Code requirements.

9. Provisions should be instituted to permit non-chargeable community facilities to be constructed on district property.

10. The state should provide incentives to local school districts to seek all financial resources available, including year-round education, relocatable classrooms, and joint use of school facilities with other community agencies.

11. The state should continue as the primary source of funds for special housing requirements for the severely handicapped (Stork, 1992).

The twelve-point program was adopted by CASH's board of directors, and the organization has been instrumental in supporting legislation to implement the plan. The organization has also supported state bond measures for school construction.

SUMMARY

In spite of the recession in California, people continue to migrate to the Golden State. Many recent immigrants have school-age children who are knocking at the doors of the state's already overcrowded schools. Districts in growing communities are challenged to build schools in a declining economic climate, and few have viable options for school construction funding.

Providing adequate school facilities in California has become a highly complex, indeed almost impossible, task. With the number of students almost doubling by 2010, the state needs to build seven new classrooms every day for the next several years to keep up with the increase in student population. Yearly cost estimates for classroom construction range from $3 to $6 billion—and increase each year.

For the past decade, the citizens of California have been asked to finance school construction by approving state facilities construction bonds. This method of financing schools has not kept pace with increases in student enrollment. Economists also warn that the state may be approaching a level of bonded indebtedness that could jeopardize the state's financial rating.

In this chapter, several alternatives for financing school construction were discussed. Each method has several disadvantages, and for most of them, gaining citizen approval generates substantial work on the part of the staff and board of education. School construction will continue to be a major challenge for the citizens of this state in the foreseeable future.

KEY TERMS

Ad valorem tax

Assessed valuation

Building permits

CASH

COPs

Deferred Maintenance Fund

Developer-donated school

Developer fees

Facilities

Funding eligibility

GO Bonds

Hart decision

Impact fees

Interim facilities

Landscape & Lighting Act

Lease/purchase program

Leroy Greene Fund

Local control

Mello-Roos Community Facilities
    District

Mira decision

Murrieta Valley decision

Office of State Architecture

Parcel Tax

Proposition 13

Proposition 46

Redevelopment Agency

Relocatable schools

Relocatables

SAB

Sales tax

Year-round schools

DISCUSSION/ESSAY QUESTIONS

1. Until the passage of Proposition 13, General Obligation Bonds were the major source of funds for school construction. What are the major advantages and disadvantages of this type of financing?

2. Certificates of Participation (COPs) have become increasingly popular with school boards as a means of financing school construction projects. What are the pro and con arguments relative to this type of financing of school construction projects?

3. The Leroy Greene Lease/Purchase legislation has been widely used to finance school construction projects. What is the funding mechanism for this program? What are the general requirements for a district to participate in the program?

4. Several California school districts that have experienced a significant increase in student enrollment have established a Mello-Roos Community Facilities District (CFD). What are the requirements for establishing a CFD? What are its advantages and disadvantages?

5. Three major court decisions regard community zoning and school enrollment: *Mira*, *Hart*, and *Murrieta Valley*. Discuss the decisions in these cases and their significance for school construction.

6. An influential lobbying group for adequate finance for school construction is the Coalition for Adequate School Housing (CASH). Who are the major players in this organization and what are their primary objectives?

Selected School Finance Terms

Abatement: Complete or partial cancellation of an expenditure or revenue. Abatement of an expenditure is the cancellation of a part or whole of a charge previously made, usually due to refunds, rebates, or resale of materials originally purchased.

Accounts Payable: Amounts due and owed to private persons, business firms, governmental units, or others for goods received by and/or services rendered to the school district prior to the end of the fiscal year; includes amounts billed, but not yet paid.

Accounts Receivable: Amounts due and owed from private persons, business firms, governmental units, or others for goods received by and/or services rendered to them prior to the end of the fiscal year; includes amounts billed, but not received.

Accrual Basis: That method of accounting in which revenue is recorded when earned, even though not collected, and expenses are recorded when liabilities are incurred, even if not yet paid.

Ad valorem: According to value. Used in taxation for a tax related to the value. For example, property tax and sales taxes are related to the value of the property or the price paid for the merchandise.

Aid to Families with Dependent Children (AFDC): A federal assistance program that provides funds to low-income families with dependent children.

Apportionment: Allocation of state or federal aid, district taxes, or other monies among LEAs or other governmental units. The first principal apportionment (P-1) is calculated in February of the school year; the second principal apportionment, in June.

Appropriation: Funds set aside or budgeted by the state or local school district for a specific time period and specific purpose.

Assembly Bill 1200: A bill passed by the legislature and approved by the governor in 1991 that imposed major fiscal accountability controls on school districts and county offices of education. This legislation established significant administrative hurdles and obligations for school district budgeting and fiscal practices. It also gave county superintendents of schools greater responsibility for and control of local district budgets.

Assessed Valuation: The value of land, homes, or businesses set by the county assessor for property tax purposes. Assessed value is either the appraised value of any newly constructed or purchased property or the value on March 1, 1975, of continuously owned property, plus an annual increase. This increase is tied to the California Consumer Price Index, but may not exceed two percent each year.

Assets: School district holdings divided into two categories. The first category is cash and that which can easily be converted into cash, such as investments and accounts receivable. The second category represents costs incurred at an earlier date that have not yet been attributed to a given period, such as buildings, depreciable equipment, prepaid expenses, and deferred charges.

Audit: An examination of documents, records, and accounts to (1) determine the propriety of transactions; (2) ascertain whether all transactions are recorded properly; and (3) determine whether statements that are drawn from accounts reflect an accurate picture of financial operations and financial status for a given period of time.

Average Daily Attendance (ADA): The number of students present or excused for absence on each school day throughout the year, divided by the total number of school days in the school year. A school district's revenue limit income is based on its ADA. (Refer to Education Code Section 46300 and California Code of Regulations, Title 5, Education, Sections 400-424.)

Basic Aid: The minimum grant of $120.00 per K-12 pupil guaranteed by the California Constitution. The amount is included in a school district's revenue limit. It is paid even in the few instances when a district's property tax income exceeds its revenue limit.

Bilingual Education: Programs for students with limited proficiency in English. Some federal and state categorical funds are provided for bilingual education.

Block Grant: A lump sum allocation of special purpose funds in which two or more special-purpose or categorical funds are lumped together for distribution to the state or LEA.

Bond: A certificate containing a written promise to pay a specified sum of money (called the face value) at a fixed time in the future (called the date of maturity) and specifying interest at a fixed rate, usually payable periodically.

Bonded Debt: That portion of indebtedness represented by outstanding bonds.

Bonded Debt Service: Expenditures that are incurred for interest on and redemption of bonds.

Budget: A plan of financial operation consisting of an estimate of proposed revenue and expenditures for a given period and purpose. The budget usually provides a financial plan for a single fiscal year.

Budget Act: The legislative vehicle for the state's budget appropriations. The state constitution requires that it be approved by a two-thirds vote of each house and sent to the governor by June 15 each year. The governor may reduce or delete, but not increase, individual items.

Capital Outlay: Amounts paid for the acquisition of fixed assets or additions to fixed assets. Fixed assets encompass land or existing buildings; improvements of grounds; construction, additions to, or remodeling of buildings; and initial purchases of or additions to equipment.

Capital Projects Funds: Funds established to account for financial resources that are to be used to acquire or construct major capital facilities.

Cash Flow: An analysis of expected cash receipts and cash disbursements. This analysis provides an anticipated cash balance for a given period of time and enables the district to know if it will be able to meet its financial obligations without borrowing money.

Cash in County Treasury: Cash balances on deposit in the county treasury for the various funds of the LEA.

California Basic Education Data System (CBEDS): Data collected from each district, usually in October each year. CBEDS includes statistical information about schools, teachers, and students. These data are used extensively by the California Department of Education and members of the state legislature in making decisions about public schools.

California Basic Education Skills Test (CBEST): A standardized test required of anyone seeking certification as a teacher, counselor, or administrator. The test measures proficiency in reading, writing, and mathematics.

Categorical Aid: Funds from the state or federal government granted to qualifying school districts for children with special needs. Examples include funds for educationally handicapped and for bilingual education. Funds may be granted also for special purposes: School Improvement Program, New Teacher Project, Mentor Teacher Program, etc. Expenditure of most categorical aid is restricted to its particular purpose. The funds are granted to districts in addition to the revenue limit.

Certificated Employees: Employees who are required by the state to hold a credential, including full-time, part-time, substitute, and temporary teachers, counselors, and administrators.

Certificates of Participation (COPs): Documents that provide long-term financing through a lease (with an option to purchase or a conditional sale agreement). They are secured by the district's General Fund.

Chart of Accounts: A list of accounts, systematically arranged, that applies to a specific LEA. All accounts are listed in numerical order with the name of each.

Class Size Penalties: Penalties imposed on school districts that have classes in excess of prescribed maximum sizes. Class size penalties result in a reduction in ADA which, in turn, results in a loss in revenue limit income. Education Code 41376 contains the class size limitations.

Classified Employees: School employees who are not required to hold teaching credentials, such as secretaries, custodians, bus drivers, food service workers, instructional aides, and some management personnel. The latter may include, for example, chief accountants, transportation directors, and directors of food service programs.

Clearing Accounts: Accounts used to accumulate total receipts or expenditures for later distribution among the accounts to which such receipts or expenditures are properly allocable.

Coefficient of Variation (CV): The standard deviation expressed as a percent of the mean. Used to compare standard deviations of varying groups of data.

Collective Bargaining: A process for negotiations between management and employees regarding salary and working conditions. Senate Bill 160, approved by the legislature in 1975, defines the manner and scope of negotiations between school districts and employee organizations.

Consumer Price Index (CPI): A measure of the cost of living compiled by the United States Bureau of Labor Statistics. These indices of inflation are calculated regularly for the United States, California, some regions within California, and selected cities. The CPI is one of several measures of economic change.

Contingent Liabilities: Items that may become liabilities as a result of conditions undetermined at a given date; e.g., guarantees, pending lawsuits, judgements and appeals, and unsettled claims.

Contra Account: An account to record offsetting transactions; e.g., abatements.

Contracted Services: Services and all related expenditures rendered under contract by personnel who are not on the payroll of the LEA.

Cost of Living Adjustment (COLA): An increase in funding for revenue limits or categorical programs. Current law ties COLAs to various indices of inflation, although different amounts are appropriated in some years.

Current Expense of Education: The current General Fund operating expenditures of an LEA for kindergarten and grades one through twelve, excluding expenditures for food services, community services, non-agency activities, fringe benefits for retired persons, facilities acquisition and construction.

Current Liabilities: Amounts due and payable for goods and services received prior to the end of the fiscal year. Current liabilities should be paid within a short period of time, usually less than a year.

Debt Service Funds: Funds established to account for accumulation of resources for, and payment of, general long-term debt principal and interest.

Deferred Maintenance: Major repairs of buildings and equipment that have been postponed by school districts. Some matching state funds are available to districts that establish a deferred maintenance program.

Deficit: The amount by which a sum of money falls short of a required amount (e.g., apportionment deficits).

Deficit Fund Balance: Within a fund, the excess of liabilities over assets.

Deficit Spending: The excess of actual expenditures over actual revenues (also referred to as an operating deficit).

Developer Fees: A specified charge per square foot on new residential and commercial construction. Developer fees are levied by school districts to generate revenues to build or renovate schools. Proceeds are used to build or renovate schools or for portable classrooms.

Direct Support Charges: Charges for a support program and services that directly benefit other programs.

Discretionary Funds: Funds allocated to a district or school that can be spent at district or site discretion.

Economic Impact Aid (EIA): State categorical aid for districts with concentrations of children who are bilingual, transient, or from low-income families.

Education Code: The body of law that regulates education in California. Additional regulations are contained in the California Administrative Code, Title 5; Government Code; and general statutes.

Education Department General Administrative Regulations (EDGAR): The regulations of the U. S. Department of Education incorporating certain circulars from the Office of Management and Budget.

Employee Benefits: Amounts paid by the LEA on behalf of employees. These amounts are over and above an individual's gross salary; they are fringe benefit payments. While not paid directly to employees, benefits nevertheless account for a portion of personnel costs. Examples are (1) group health or life insurance payments, (2) contributions to employee retirement, (3) OASDI (social security) taxes, (4) workers' compensation payments, and (5) payments made to personnel on sabbatical leave.

Encroachment: The expenditure of a school district's general purpose funds for special purpose programs, such as special education or transportation. Encroachment occurs in most districts that provide services for handicapped children. Other common examples of encroachment include student food services and student transportation.

Encumbrances: Obligations in the form of purchase orders, contracts, salaries, and other commitments chargeable to an appropriation and for which a part of the appropriation is reserved.

Enterprise Funds: Funds used to account for those ongoing LEA activities that, because of their income-producing character, are similar to activities in the private sector.

Equalization: Funds allocated by the legislature to raise districts with lower revenue limits toward the statewide average.

Expenditures: The costs of goods delivered or services rendered, whether paid or unpaid, including expenses, provision for debt retirement not reported as a liability of the fund from which retired, and capital outlay.

Fidelity Bond: A form of insurance that provides for indemnification of the LEA or other employer for losses arising from theft by or dishonesty of employees.

Financial Management and Accountability Committee (FMAC): A committee formed within the California Department of Education to review and redesign financial reporting forms for all school districts. The FMAC accounting system was required of all districts and county offices of education as of the 1988-89 school year.

Fiscal Year: A period of one year, the beginning and the ending dates of which are fixed by statute. In California, the fiscal year begins on July 1 and ends on June 30.

Fixed Assets: Assets of a permanent character having continuing value; e.g., land, buildings, machinery, furniture, and equipment.

Full-time equivalent: The ratio derived by dividing the number of work hours required in a part-time position by the number of work hours required in a corresponding full-time position.

Fund: A fiscal and accounting entity with a self-balancing set of accounts recording cash and other financial resources, together with all related liabilities and residual equities or balances, and changes therein, which are segregated to carry on specific activities or attain certain objectives in accordance with applicable regulations, restrictions, or limitations.

Fund Balance: The difference between assets and liabilities; the fund equity of governmental and trust funds.

Gann Spending Limit: A ceiling, or limit, on each year's appropriation of tax dollars by the state, cities, counties, school districts, and special districts. Districts are permitted to increase budgets equal to inflation—that is, equal to the change in the Consumer Price Index or per capita personal income, whichever is smaller—or changes in the district's ADA. Proposition 111, adopted in June 1990, amended the Gann inflation factor to equate only to the change in per capita personal income.

General Fund: The fund used to finance the ordinary operations of the LEA. It is available for any legally authorized purpose.

General Obligation Bonds: Bonds for capital outlay, financed through taxes. Elections to authorize General Obligation Bonds in a school district must be approved by a two-thirds vote. State measures only require a majority vote.

Generally Accepted Accounting Principles (GAAP): Uniform minimum standards of, and guidelines for, financial accounting and reporting. These accounting principles govern the form and content of the basic financial statements of an entity. They encompass the conventions, rules, and procedures necessary to define accepted accounting practices at a particular time. They include not only broad guidelines of general application, but also detailed practices and procedures. Generally accepted accounting principles provide a standard against which to measure financial presentations. The primary authoritative source on application of these principles to state and local governments is the Governmental Accounting Standards Board (GASB).

Grants-in-Aid: Outright donations or contributions, usually by a superior governmental unit, without prior establishment of conditions with which the recipient must comply.

Holding Accounts: Suspense accounts that are used temporarily to accumulate costs that will ultimately be charged to other programs.

Income: A term used in accounting for a proprietary fund type to represent the excess of revenues earned over the expenses incurred in carrying on the fund's operations. The term "income" should not be used in lieu of revenue in governmental-type funds.

Indirect Cost and Overhead: Elements of cost necessary in operating an LEA or in performing a service that are of such nature that the amount applicable to each accounting unit cannot be determined readily and accurately or for which the cost of such determination exceeds the benefit of the determination.

Indirect Support Charges: Charges for routine services not performed as a special service for a particular program, but allocated to using programs.

Interfund Transfers: Money that is taken from one fund under the control of the governing board and added to another fund under the board's control. Interfund transfers are not revenues or expenditures of the LEA; they simply move dollars from one fund to another.

Internal Audit: An appraisal activity within an LEA that (1) determines the adequacy of the system of internal control, (2) verifies and safeguards assets, (3) determines the reliability of the accounting and reporting system, (4) ascertains compliance with existing policies and procedures, and (5) appraises the performance of activities and work programs.

Internal Control: A plan of organization under which employees' duties are so arranged and records and procedures so designed as to provide a system of self-checking, thereby enhancing accounting control over assets, liabilities, revenue, and expenditures. Under such a system employees' work is subdivided so no one employee performs a complete cycle of operation; such procedures call for proper authorization by designated officials.

Intrabudget Transfers: Amounts transferred from one appropriation account to another within the same fund.

Inventory: A detailed list showing quantities and description of property on hand at a given time. It also may include units of measure, unit prices, and values.

J-200, J-380: Financial and program cost accounting reports submitted by districts and county offices to the California Department of Education. The information is used to monitor the fiscal conditions of districts.

LEP (Limited-English-Proficient): LEP students are those who do not have fluent English language skills (i.e., comprehension, speaking, reading, and writing) necessary to succeed in the school's regular instructional program. LEP includes non-English-speaking and limited-English-proficient students.

Lease-Purchase Agreements: Contractual agreements that are termed "leases," but, in substance, amount to purchase contracts.

Liabilities: Legal obligations (with the exception of encumbrances) that are unpaid.

Life Span (grade span): Broad group classification of students according to age and school progress, i.e., preformal, elementary, secondary, and adult.

Local Educational Agency (LEA): The local school district.

Lottery: A game of chance approved by California voters in 1984. A minimum of 34% of lottery revenues is distributed to public schools and colleges and must be used for education of pupils.

Maintenance Assessment Districts: School districts acting under legislation that permits charging property owners a fee for improvement of school playgrounds and athletic fields. Districts may impose the "fee" by a vote of the local governing board, but the district must show a benefit to each fee payer.

Mandated Costs: School district expenditures that occur as a result of federal or state law, court decisions, administrative regulations, or initiative measures. School districts are eligible to apply for state funds to reimburse these costs.

Mean: The arithmetic average of data.

Median: The middle number in a group when data are arranged in numeric sequence.

Mega-Item: Block funding for selected categorical programs. The procedure was initiated in 1992-93 and allows districts to redirect a portion of categorical funds from one categorical program to another.

Mello-Roos: A community facilities district that can be established by a two-thirds vote to issue bonds and levy local taxes for school construction.

Mentor Teacher: A specially selected teacher who receives a stipend to work with new and experienced teachers on curriculum and instruction.

Migrant Education: Special funds for districts with students who are children of migrant workers.

Modified Accrual Basis: The accrual basis of accounting adapted to the governmental fund type. Under it, revenues are recognized when they become both "measurable" and "available" to finance expenditures of the current period. Most expenditures are recognized (recorded) when the related liability is incurred.

Multi-year Financial Plan: A plan that presents in tabular form financial estimates of program costs over a period of years. These estimates should reflect future financial impact of current decisions. The data in the plan should be organized to be consistent with program structure.

Necessary Small School: An elementary school with less than 101 ADA or a high school with less than 301 ADA that meets the standards "necessary."

Object: As used in an expenditure classification, a term that applies to the article purchased or the service obtained.

Parcel Tax: A special tax that is not *ad valorem* (proportional to the value of the property). Usually the tax is for a specific purpose. Parcel taxes must be approved by local two-thirds vote.

Permissive Override Tax: A tax authorized prior to Proposition 13, allowing a school district governing board to levy a special tax for the improvement of education. Districts are no longer allowed to levy such taxes.

Prepaid Expenses: Items for which payment has been made, but from which benefits have not been realized as of a certain date; e.g., prepaid rent, prepaid interest, and premiums on unexpired insurance.

Prior Year's Taxes: Tax revenues that were delinquent in a prior year and are received in the current fiscal year. In the revenue limit formula, these revenues offset state aid for the current year.

Property Taxes: Taxes based on ownership of property and measured by its value. Property taxes include both general property taxes (i.e., relating to property as a whole, real or personal, tangible or intangible, whether taxed at a single rate or at classified rates) and special property taxes (i.e., on selected types of property, such as motor vehicles or certain or all tangibles, subject to rates that are not directly related to rates applying to general property taxation).

Proposition 13: An initiative amendment passed in 1978 adding Article XIII A to the California Constitution. Tax rates on secured property are restricted to a maximum of one percent of full cash value. Proposition 13 also defined assessed value and requires a two-thirds vote to change existing taxes or levying of new taxes.

Public Employees' Retirement System (PERS): A California state retirement system established for state employees. California school classified employees are members of PERB.

Public Employment Relations Board (PERB): A board of five persons appointed by the governor to regulate collective bargaining between school employers and employee organizations.

Range: The difference between the highest and lowest values in a group of data.

Real Property: Property consisting of land, buildings, minerals, timber, landscaping, and all improvements thereto.

Regional Occupational Center or Program (ROC/P): A vocational education program for high school students and adults. An ROC or ROP may be operated by a single district, by a consortium of districts under a joint powers agreement, or by a county office of education for districts within that county.

Registered Warrant: A warrant that is registered by the county treasurer for future payment because of present lack of funds. Registered warrants are to be paid with interest in the order of their registration.

Reserves: Funds set aside in a school district budget to provide for future expenditures or to offset future losses, for working capital, or for other purposes.

Restricted Funds: Monies whose use is restricted by legal requirements or by a donor. These funds can only be spent for a specific purpose or program. Funds received in excess of the expenditures in any one year must be carried over to the next year for that program or returned to the donor (state or other source of funds).

Revenue Limit: The specific amount of state and local taxes a school district may receive per pupil for its general education program. Annual increases are determined by the legislature. Categorical aid is allocated in addition to the revenue limit.

Revenues: Increases in fund financial resources other than interfund transfers or debt issue proceeds. Revenues are the primary financial resource of a fund. Revenues are recognized when assets are increased without increasing liabilities or incurring an obligation to repay expenditures.

Revolving Cash Fund: A stated amount of money used primarily for emergency or small disbursements and reimbursed periodically through properly documented expenditures, which are summarized and charged to proper accounting classifications.

School Improvement Program (SIP): Money granted by the state to selected schools to carry out a plan developed by the school site council for improvement of the school's program.

School Site Council: Parents, students, teachers, and other staff selected by their peers to prepare a school improvement plan and to assist in seeing that planned activities are carried out and evaluated.

Scope of Bargaining: The range of subjects negotiated between school districts and employee organizations during the collective bargaining process. Scope includes matters relating to wages, hours, and working conditions. PERB is responsible for interpreting disputes as to matters that are or are not within scope.

Second Period Attendance (P-2): The period of time from July 1 through the last full school month ending on or before April 15. Revenue limit sources are based on ADA generated during this period.

Secured Roll: Assessed value of real property, such as land, buildings, secured personal property, or anything permanently attached to land, as determined by each county assessor.

Senate Bill 90: Finance legislation approved by the legislature and signed by the governor in 1972. This legislation established the revenue limit system for funding school districts. The first revenue limit amount was determined by dividing the district's 1972-73 state and local income by that year's ADA. This per-ADA amount is the historical base for all subsequent revenue limit calculations.

Senate Bill 813: Education reform legislation approved by the legislature and signed by the governor in 1983. This legislation contained a series of "reforms" in funding calculations, as well as in programs. Longer day, longer year, mentor teachers, and beginning teacher salary adjustment are a few of the programs implemented by SB 813.

Serrano v. Priest: A California Supreme Court decision that declared the system of financing schools unconstitutional because it violated the equal protection clause of the state's constitution. The court said that by 1980 the relative effort, or tax rate, required of taxpayers for local schools must be nearly the same throughout the state and that differences in annual per-pupil expenditures due to local wealth must be less than $100.00. The impact of Proposition 13 settled the taxpayer equity provision.

Shortfall: An insufficient allocation of money, requiring an additional appropriation or resulting in deficits.

Split Roll: A system for taxing business and industrial property at a different rate from individual homeowners.

Squeeze Formula: The formula used from 1973-1974 through 1981-1982 to calculate the annual inflation increase in the base revenue limit. This calculation provided smaller-than-average increases to high-revenue districts, thus "squeezing" their revenues as a means of accomplishing revenue equalization. Effective in 1983-1984 the squeeze formula was eliminated; since then, all districts of the same type now receive the same dollar inflation increase.

Standard Deviation (SDEV): A statistical technique measuring the extent to which data vary from their mean. Used to indicate the relative dispersion of individual items.

State Allocation Board (SAB): A regulatory agency that controls most state-aided capital outlay and deferred maintenance projects and distributes funds for them.

State School Fund: A fund to which the state appropriates money each year. The monies are then used to make state aid payments to school districts. Section A of the State School Fund is for K-12 education; Section B, for community college education.

State Teachers' Retirement System (STRS): A state retirement system for teachers and other certificated employees. State law requires certificated employees, school districts, and the state to contribute to this retirement system.

Stores: Goods that are on hand in storerooms and subject to requisition.

Sunset: The termination of regulations for a categorical program. A schedule for the legislature to consider the sunset of most state programs is in current law. The law was intended to ensure the evaluation of programs on a regular time interval so those no longer useful could be discontinued.

Tax Anticipation Notes: Notes issued in anticipation of collection of taxes, usually retirable only from tax collections and frequently only from the proceeds of the tax levy whose collection they anticipate.

Tax Relief Subventions: Funds ordinarily paid to compensate for taxes lost because of tax relief measures.

Tenure: A system of due process and employment guarantee for teachers. After serving a two-year probation period, teachers are assured continued employment in the school district unless very carefully defined procedures for dismissal or layoff are successfully followed.

Tidelands Oil Revenues: Money for oil on state-owned lands. When available, some of the revenues are appropriated for K-12 capital outlay needs or other special purposes.

Transfer: Interdistrict or interfund payments or receipts not chargeable to expenditures or credited to revenue. Certain budget revisions are often referred to as transfers.

Unencumbered Balance: That portion of an appropriation or allotment not yet expended or obligated.

Unification: Joining together of all or part of an elementary school district (K-6 or K-8) and high school district (7-12 or 9-12) to form a new unified school district (K-12) with a single governing board.

Unified School District: A school district serving students from kindergarten through 12th grade.

Unrestricted Funds: Funds received for the general education of students. These funds are also used for support costs necessary to operate a school district. The majority of unrestricted revenues come from the revenue limit calculation that is based on the district's ADA. Lottery funds are also unrestricted.

Unsecured Roll: Assessed value of personal property other than secured property.

Urban Impact/Meade Aid: State aid to large, metropolitan districts and to qualifying high school and their feeder elementary districts. The money carries no restrictions on its use. This legislation was approved on the assumption that the cost of education is higher in a metropolitan area than elsewhere.

Vouchers: Coupons issued by a state to individual children for admission to school and redeemed by those schools for cash. A voucher system could include public as well as private school students.

Waiver: Permission from the California Board of Education in response to the request of a school district to set aside the requirements of an Education Code provision.

Work Order: A written authorization for performance of a particular job. A work order describes the nature and location of the job and specifies the work to be performed. Such authorizations are usually assigned job numbers, and provision is made for accumulating and reporting labor, material, and other costs.

References

ACLU sues state over conditions in poor schools. (2000, May 18) *Los Angeles Times.*

ACSA (Association of California School Administrators). (1998) Governor Pete Wilson's State of the State Address. (Online: http://www.acsa.org/publications/social _promotion)

Agreement ends 20-year struggle to recoup special education costs. (2000, November) *California Educator 5*(3).

Atkinson, Andelson, Loya, Rudd & Romo. (1992, April 3) California Supreme Court decision affirms legality of assessing a fee for home-to-school transportation. File Reference Memo #57. San Bernardino, CA: Author.

Barner, R. (1999) (Online: http://www.ed.gov/publications/social_promotion)

Benson, C. S. (1978) *The economics of public education.* 3rd ed. Boston: Houghton Mifflin.

Black, H. C. (1991) *Black's law dictionary*, 6th ed. St. Paul, MN: West Publishing.

Bowie, A. (1992, March 24) Schools—Who will pay? *Proceedings of the Convention of the Building Industry Association of Southern California.*

Boyer, E. J. (1996, November 21) Rising number of state schools offer breakfasts. *Los Angeles Times.*

Bracey, G. W. (1995) Debunking the myths about money for schools. *Educational Leadership, 53*(3).

Brittan, E., Consultant in Business Advisory Services for San Bernardino County Superintendent of Schools, Administration and Business Division. (1992) Interview. San Bernardino, CA.

Bustillos, T. A. (1989, September) Expectations held for the California school business administrator. *California Association of School Business Officials Journal, 54.*

CalFacts (2000). Program trends. (Online: http://www.lao.ca.gov/2000_reports/calfacts/2000 _calfacts_program_trends)

California Association of School Business Officials. (1988) Legal aspects and accounting for student organizations and booster clubs. Workshop presented by the CASBO Professional Development Committee.

California Department of Education. (1983) *Report: Financial Management Advisory Committee.* Sacramento, CA: Author.

California Department of Education. (1992a) *Accounting procedures for student organizations.* Sacramento, CA: Author.

California Department of Education. (1992b) *California school accounting manual.* Sacramento, CA: Author.

California Department of Education. (1995) *1990-1995 lists of food service consultants and management contracts in public schools.* Compiled by the Child Nutrition and Food Distribution Division. Sacramento, CA: Author. (Online: http://www.cde.ca.gov)

California Department of Education. (2000a) *CBEDS: 1999-2000.* Sacramento, CA: Author. (Online: http://www.cde.ca.gov/demographics/files/cbedshome.htm)

California Department of Education. (2000b) Education in California. (Online: http://www. dof.ca.gov/html/budgetOO-1,K-12-N.htm)

California Department of Education. (2001) Data-Quest. Sacramento, CA: Author. (Online: http://data1.cde.ca.gov/dataquest/)

California Lottery Commission. (2000) *California state lottery, total K-12 annual lottery allocation per ADA.* Sacramento, CA: Author.

California public school directory (2000). Sacramento, CA: California Department of Education.

California school accounting manual. (2000). Sacramento, CA: California Department of Education. (Online: http://www.cde.ca.gov/fiscal/sacs/csam2000/csam2000full.pdf)

California School Food Service Association. (1994, December) Information packet provided at the California School Boards Association Annual Meeting, San Diego, CA.

REFERENCES

Caton, J. (1990) *The history of the American School Food Service Association: A pinch of love*. Alexandria, VA: American School Food Service Association.

Caughey, J. W. (1943) *California*. 2nd ed. Englewood Cliffs, NJ: Prentice-Hall.

Children Now. (1996) California: The state of our children: Report card '96. Author. (Online: http://www.childrennow.org/california/RC_96/rc96.htm)

Colvin, R. L., & Lesher, D. (1997, July 22) Governor denies tax would harm education. *Los Angeles Times*.

Connell, K. (2000) *Annual financial report of California schools*. Sacramento, CA: Controller of the State of California. (Online: http://www.sco.ca.gov/aud/k-12 audit/2000/k-12aud.pdf)

Department of Corrections. (2000, February 17) Population projections, 1995-2005. Sacramento, CA: The Author. (Online: http://www.cdc.state.ca.us/pd/sooproj.pdf)

Donahue, P. L. (2000) The Nation's report card. Washington, DC: National Assessment of Educational Progress. (Online: http://www.nces.ed.gov)

Driftmier, D. (1997, February 7) Presentation at ACSA School Business Managers Academy.

Duffy, T. G. (1990) Finding the funds. *Thrust for Educational Leadership, 20*:259-264.

Ed-Data. (2000) A snapshot of the California public school system. (Online: http://www.ed-data.k12.ca.us)

EdSource. (1998a) California's school facilities predicament. Palo Alto, CA: Author.

EdSource. (1998b) How California compares. Palo Alto, CA: Author.

EdSource. (2001) How California ranks. Palo Alto, CA: Author.

Education Week Magazine. (1999, September) Technology counts (Special issue).

Elias, T. D. (2000, March 13) California kills majority rule. *North County Times*.

Federal Food Programs. (20010 Federal Research and Action Center. (Online: http://www.frac.org/html/federal_food_programs/programs/nslp.html)

Fellmeth, R. C. & Weichel, E. D. (2001) California Children's Budget 2000-2001. Sacramento, CA: Children's Advocacy Institute.

Goldfinger, P. (2001) *Revenue and limits.* Sacramento, CA: School Services of California.

Gorton, R. A. (1983) *School administration and supervision.* 2nd ed. Dubuque, IA: Wm. C. Brown.

Governor's Office (1999, January 6) State of the state address. (Online: http://www.governor.ca.gov/state/govsite/gov_speeches_details.jsp)

Grimes, A. (2000, September 23) Internet is hotbed of online education. *North County Times*, D6.

Groves, M. (2000, December 17). Exit exam retreats reflect fears that students lack skills. *Los Angeles Times.*

Hartman, W. T. (1988) *School district budgeting.* Englewood Cliffs, NJ: Prentice Hall.

Helfland, D. (2000a, February 8) Bill will force U. S. to cover 40% of special education, *Los Angeles Times.*

Helfland, D. (2000b, December 28) Group plans to launch online K-12 curriculum. *Los Angeles Times*, A4.

Herdt, T. (1997, July 8). Paying for schools bedevils lawmakers. *The Star.*

Hill, E. (2000)The 2001-02 Budget: Perspectives and issues. Sacramento, CA: Legislative Analyst's Office. (Online: http://www.lao.ca.gov/analysis_2001/2001_pandi/pandi_toc_anl2001.html)

Hill, E. (2001) California spending plan 2001-02: The budget act and related legislation. Sacramento, CA: Legislative Analyst (Online: http://www.lao.ca.gov/2001/spend_plan_/0901_spend_plan.pdf)

Hirano, S. (1999, December) 25 events that shaped school transportation. *School Bus Fleet.* (Online: http://www.schoolbusfleet.com/ [search the archives])

Jeffers, M. (2000, Summer) Exercising healthy choices. *CASBO Journal, 65*(2).

Kelly, K. (1999, January-February) Retention vs. social promotion, *Harvard Education Newsletter*. (Online: http://www.edletter.org/past/issues/1999-jf/retention.shtml)

Legislative Analyst's Office. (2001, May 1) A new blueprint for California school facility finance. (Online: http://www.lao.ca.gov)

Legislative update. (1996, August 6) San Bernardino, CA: San Bernardino County Superintendent of Schools.

McCann, S. (1995) *Privatization of school food services and its effect on the financial status of the Cafeteria Fund in participating California public school districts.* Unpublished Dissertation, Pepperdine University.

Malone, J. (1998, Spring) The CFO in the twenty-first century, *CASBO Journal, 63:1.*

Melendez, M. (1991) Looking ahead. *Thrust for Educational Leadership, 20:54*, April.

Mitchell, D. E. & Treiman, J. E. (1993) School district reform. Riverside, CA: California Educational Research Cooperative.

Modernizing our schools: What will it cost? (2000). Washington, DC: National Education Association. (Online: http://www.nea.org/lac/modern/modrpt.pdf)

National Association of State Directors of Pupil Transportation Services. (2000) (Online: http://www.nasdpts.org/paperCrashProtect.html)

National Center for Education Statistics. (2000) Age of school buildings. The Author. (Online: http://www.nces.ed.gov/pubs2000)

National Center for Education Statistics. (2001) NAEP state profiles. The Author. (Online: http://www.nces.ed.gov/nationsreportcard/states)

National Highway Traffic Safety Administration (2000) (Online: http://www.nhtsa.org/people/injury/buses)

Next spring's high school exit exam should concern educators at all levels. (2000, November) *California Educator, 5*(3).

North County Times (2000, September 23)

Oswalt, S. (1992) Fiscal fiascos. *Thrust for Educational Leadership, 22*(3).

Pre-1977 U. S. school buses. (2000) *School Bus Fleet*. (Online: http://www.schoolbusfleet. com/SBFFB01p62.pdf)

Rothstein, R. (1995, Summer). Where has the money gone? *Rethinking Schools, 6.*

Saunders, R. P., Fee, M., & Gottlieb, N. H. (1999, January) Higher education and the health of America's children: Collaborating for coordinated school health, *Phi Delta Kappan, 80:*377-382.

Savage, D. G. (1992, June 19) U. S. justices uphold Proposition 13 tax structure. *Los Angeles Times.*

School transportation 1997-98 school year. (2000) *School Bus Fleet Magazine.* (Online: http://www.schoolbusfleet.com/stat_1_1.cfm)

Scott, J. (1990) Seminar for school district and community college business office personnel and school district auditors. San Bernardino, CA.

Stork, F. C. (1992) Back to the drawing board. *Thrust for Educational Leadership, 21*(6): 38-41.

Tamaki, J. (2000, May 4) State population rises 571,000 with Southland in lead. *Los Angeles Times.*

Texas Department of Education. (2000) (Online: http://www.tea.state.tx.us)

U. S. Bureau of the Census (2000). (Online: http://www.census.gov)

Voters will get a chance to fix the state's schools. (1999, November) *California Educator* *4*(3).

Wainer, H. (1993, December) Does spending money on education help? *Educational Researcher 22*(9): 22-24.

White, K. (1997, February 26) Reporter's notebook: School funding gets put under states' microscope. *Education Week on the Web, 1.*

Winton, R. (2000, October 25) Parents sue district, seek refund of fees. *Los Angeles Times.*

INDEX